FOR ORGANS, PIANOS & ELECTRONIC KEYBOARDS

E-Z PLAY TODAY

9

CHRISTMAS TIME
2ND EDITION

ISBN 978-1-4950-9617-4

HAL•LEONARD®
7777 W. BLUEMOUND RD. P.O. BOX 13819 MILWAUKEE, WI 53213

In Australia Contact:
Hal Leonard Australia Pty. Ltd.
4 Lentara Court
Cheltenham, Victoria, 3192 Australia
Email: ausadmin@halleonard.com.au

E-Z Play® Today Music Notation © 1975 by HAL LEONARD LLC
E-Z PLAY and EASY ELECTRONIC KEYBOARD MUSIC are registered trademarks of HAL LEONARD LLC.

Visit Hal Leonard Online at
www.halleonard.com

Angels from the Realms of Glory

Registration 2
Rhythm: March

Words by James Montgomery
Music by Henry T. Smart

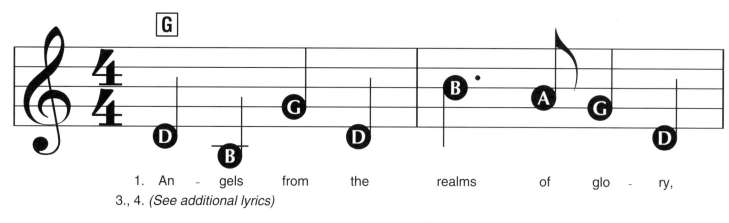

1. An - gels from the realms of glo - ry,
3., 4. *(See additional lyrics)*

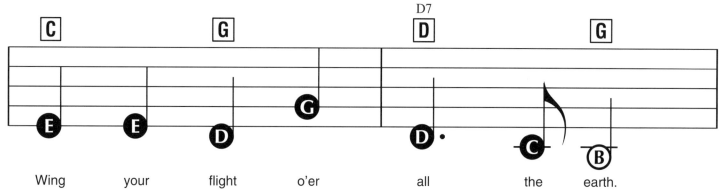

Wing your flight o'er all the earth.

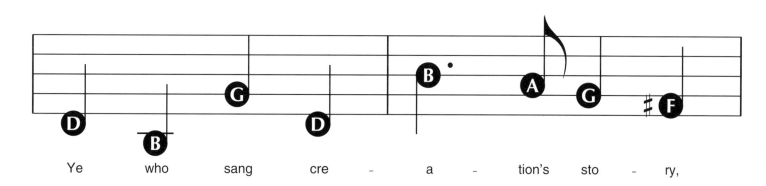

Ye who sang cre - a - tion's sto - ry,

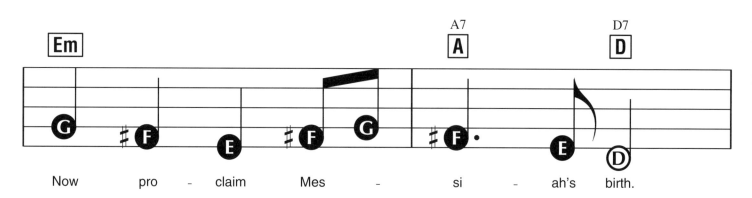

Now pro - claim Mes - si - ah's birth.

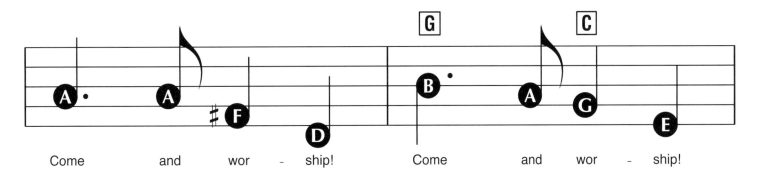

Come and wor - ship! Come and wor - ship!

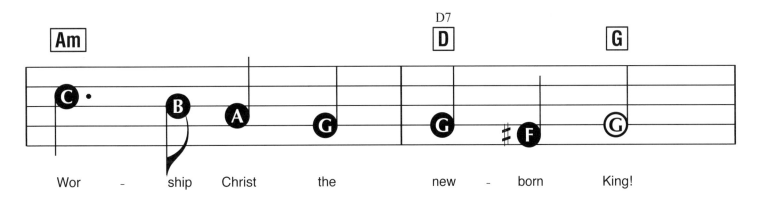

Wor - ship Christ the new - born King!

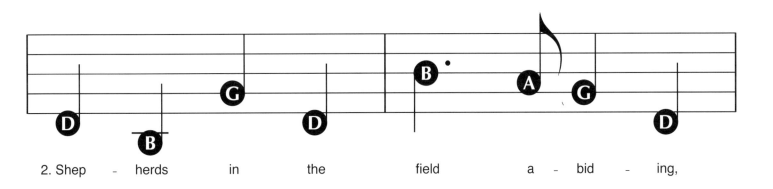

2. Shep - herds in the field a - bid - ing,

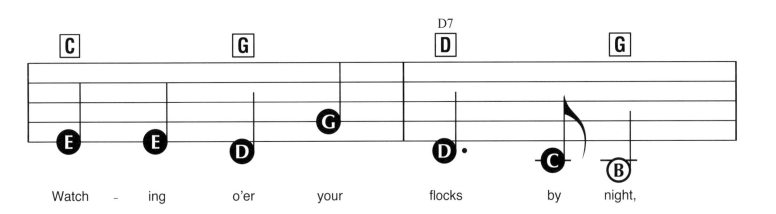

Watch - ing o'er your flocks by night,

4

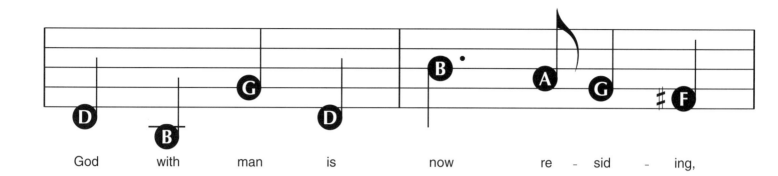

God with man is now re - sid - ing,

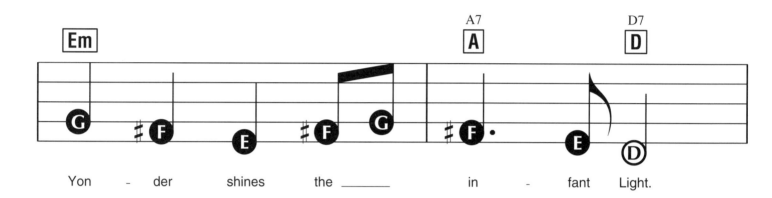

Yon - der shines the _____ in - fant Light.

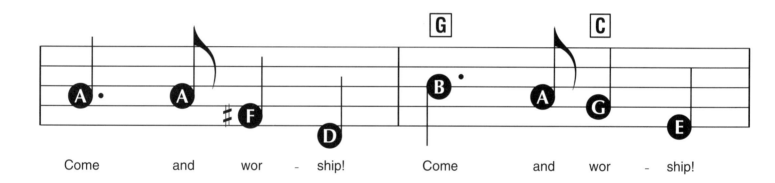

Come and wor - ship! Come and wor - ship!

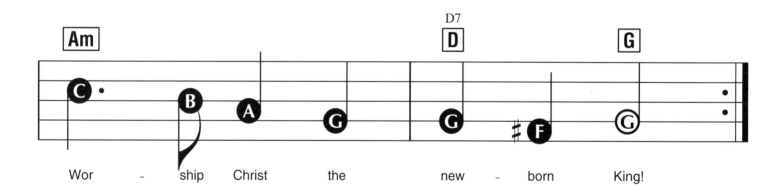

Wor - ship Christ the new - born King!

Additional Lyrics

3. Sages, leave your contemplations,
   Brighter visions beam afar.
   Seek the great Desire of Nations.
   Ye have seen His natal star.

   Come and worship!
   Come and worship!
   Worship Christ the newborn King!

4. Saints before the altar bending,
   Watching long in hope and fear.
   Suddenly the Lord, descending,
   In His temple shall appear.

   Come and worship!
   Come and worship!
   Worship Christ, the newborn King!

Angels We Have Heard on High

Registration 6
Rhythm: March or None

Traditional French Carol
Translated by James Chadwick

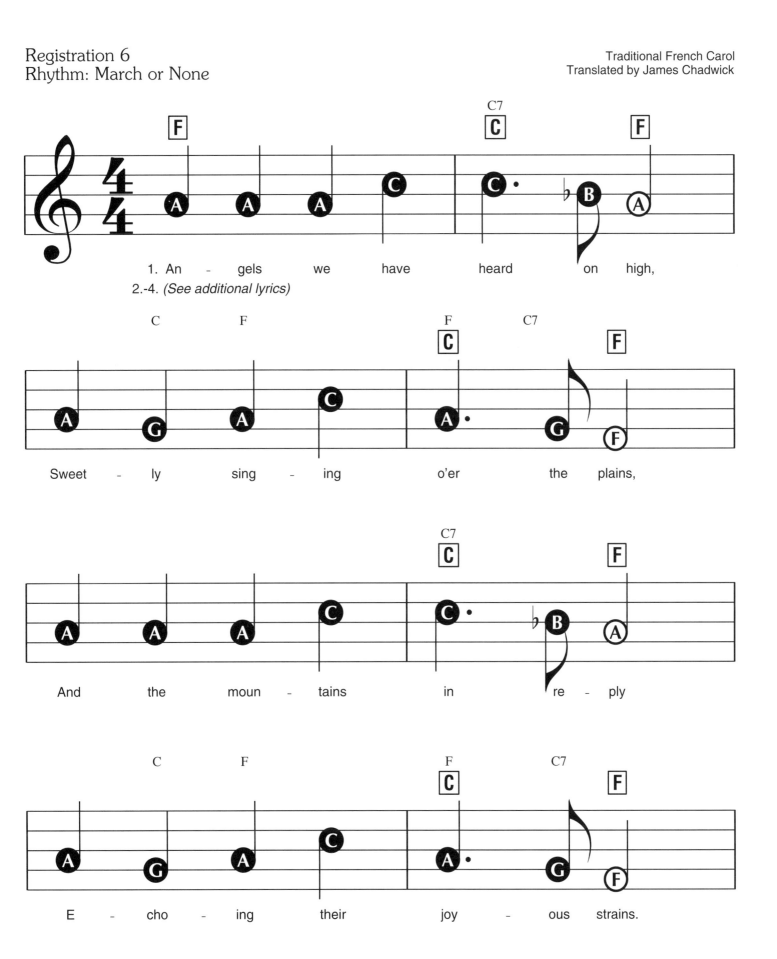

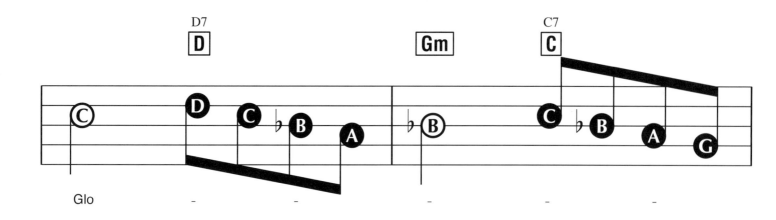

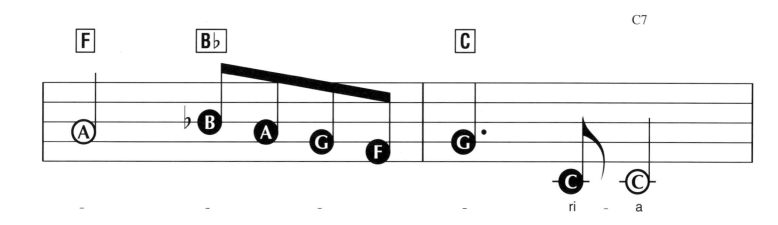

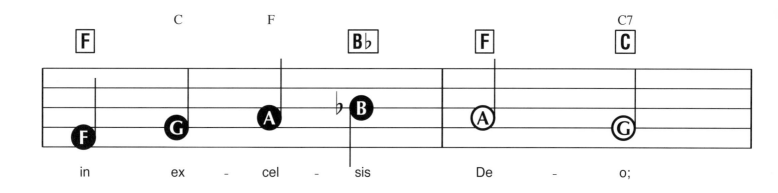

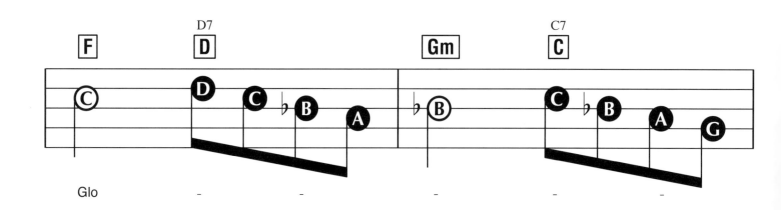

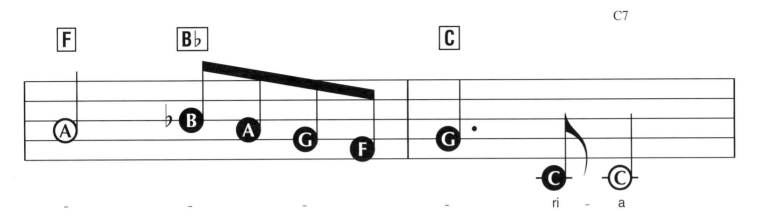

ri - a

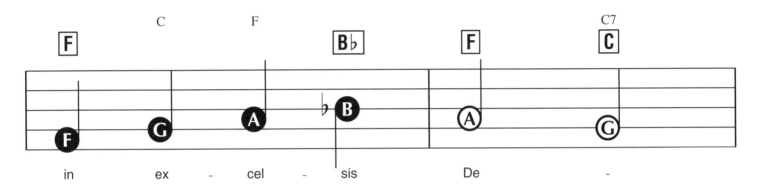

in ex - cel - sis De -

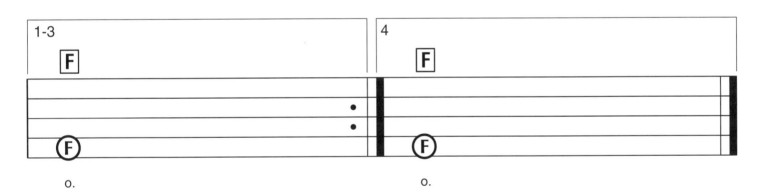

o. o.

Additional Lyrics

2. Shepherds, why this jubilee?
   Why your joyous strains prolong?
   Say what may the tidings be
   Which inspire your heavenly song?

   Gloria in excelsis Deo;
   Gloria in excelsis Deo.

3. Come to Bethlehem and see
   Him whose birth the angels sing.
   Come, adore on bended knee,
   Christ, the Lord, the newborn King.

   Gloria in excelsis Deo;
   Gloria in excelsis Deo.

4. See Him in a manger laid,
   Whom the choirs of angels praise;
   Mary, Joseph, lend your aid,
   While our hearts in love we raise.

   Gloria in excelsis Deo;
   Gloria in excelsis Deo.

As with Gladness Men of Old

Registration 10
Rhythm: None

Words by William Chatterton Dix
Music by Conrad Kocher

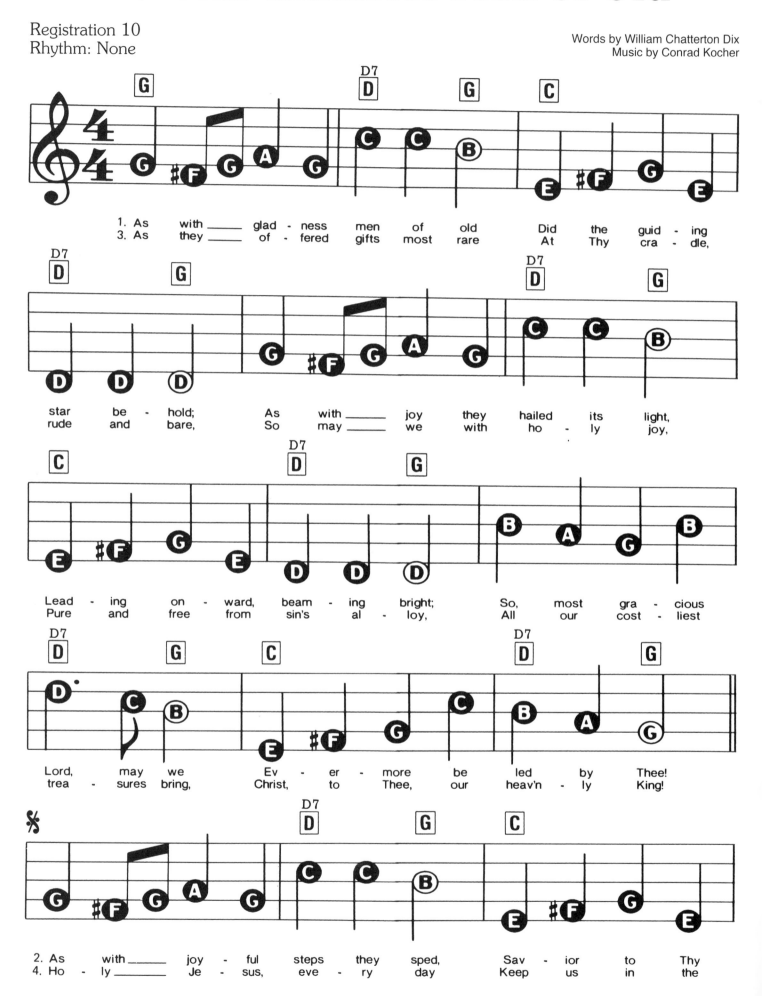

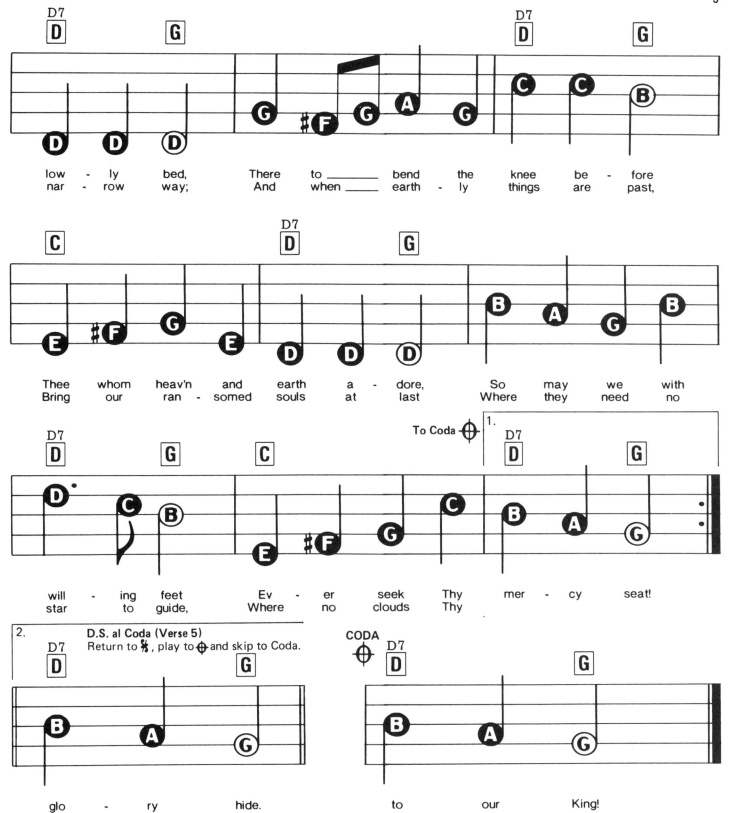

5. In the heavenly country bright
Need they no created light;
Thou its Light, its Joy, its Crown,
Thou its Sun which goes not down.
There forever may we sing
Alleluias to our King!

Auld Lang Syne

Registration 2
Rhythm: None

Words by Robert Burns
Traditional Scottish Melody

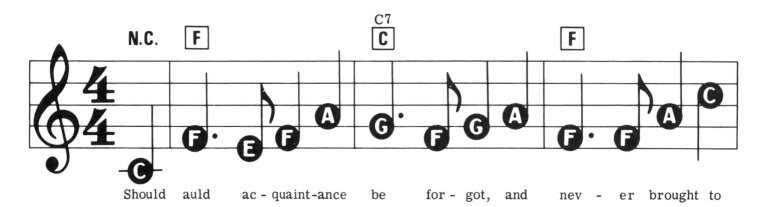

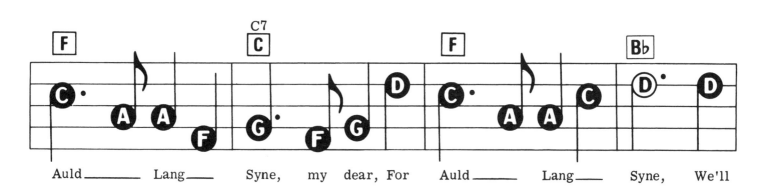

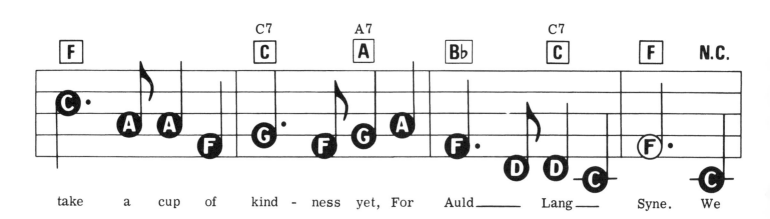

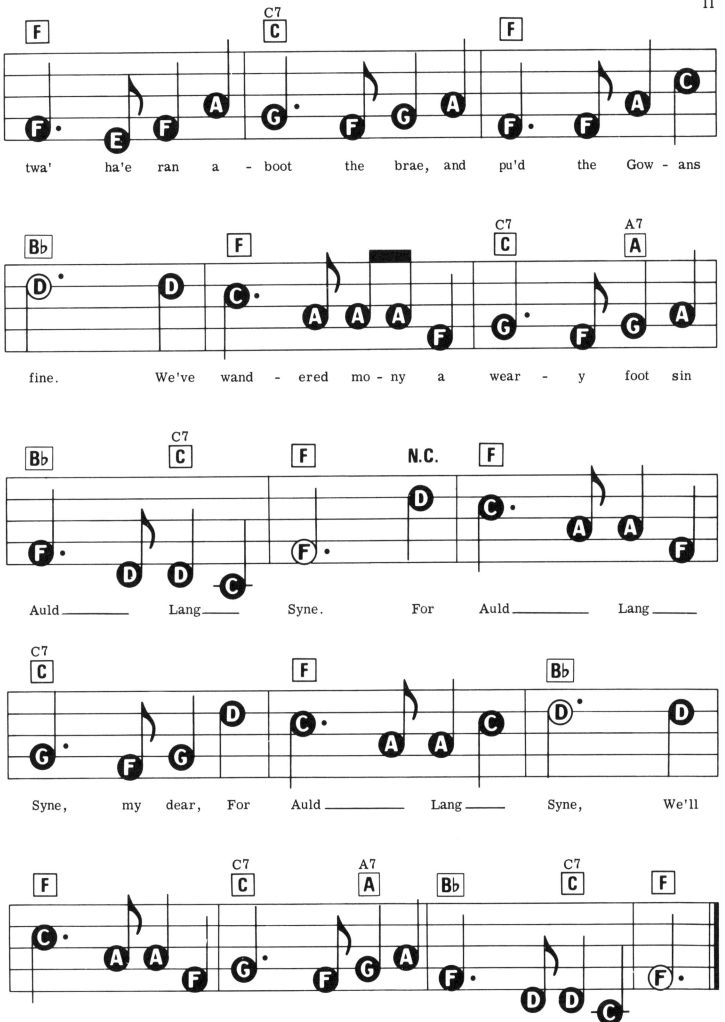

Away in a Manger

Registration 1
Rhythm: Waltz

Words by John T. McFarland (v.3)
Music by James R. Murray

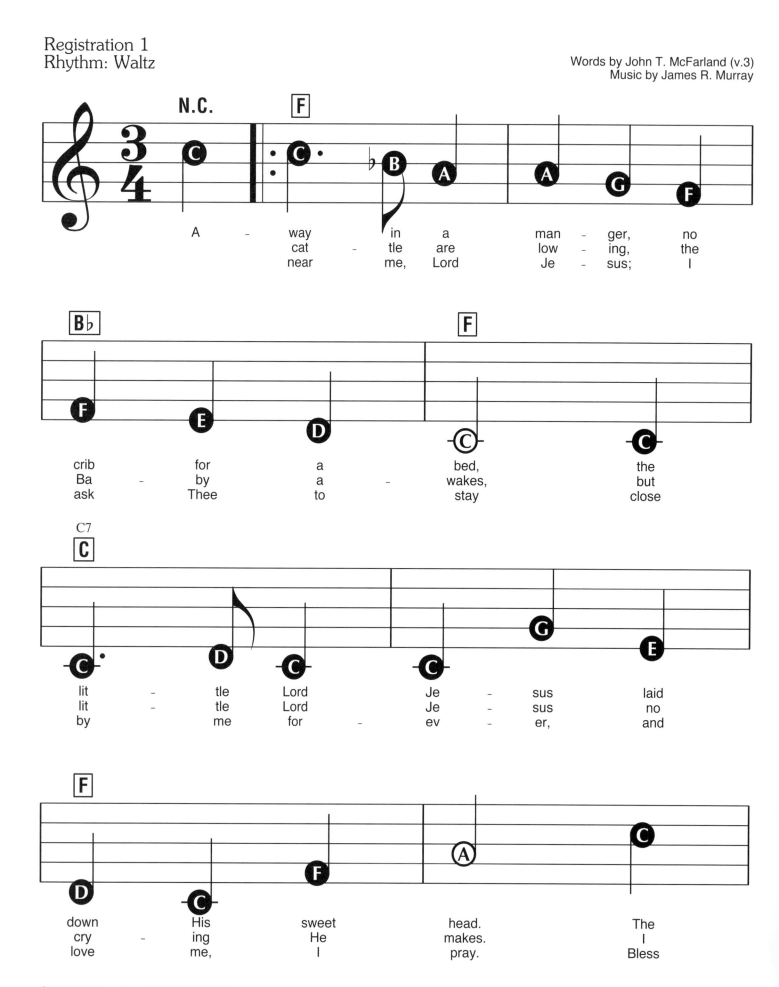

13

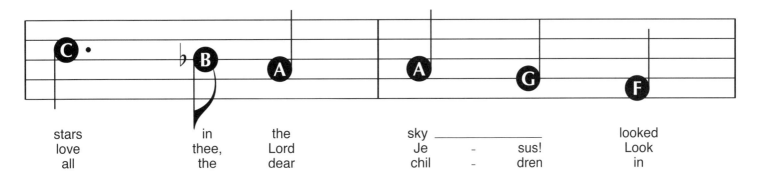

stars   in   the   sky _____ looked
love   thee,   Lord   Je - sus!   Look
all   the   dear   chil - dren   in

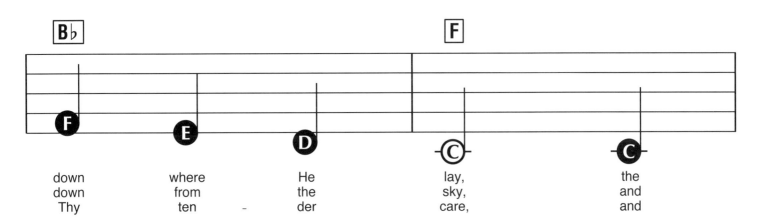

down   where   He   lay,   the
down   from   the   sky,   and
Thy   ten - der   care,   and

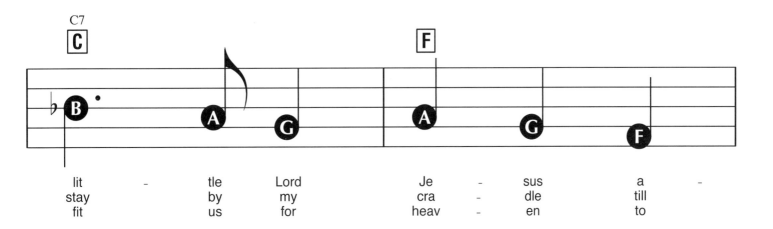

lit - tle   Lord   Je - sus   a -
stay   by   my   cra - dle   till
fit   us   for   heav - en   to

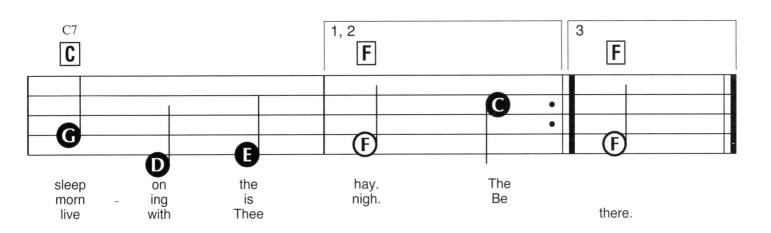

sleep   on   the   hay.   The
morn - ing   is   nigh.   Be
live   with   Thee   there.

Bring a Torch, Jeannette, Isabella

Registration 3
Rhythm: Waltz

17th Century French Provençal Carol

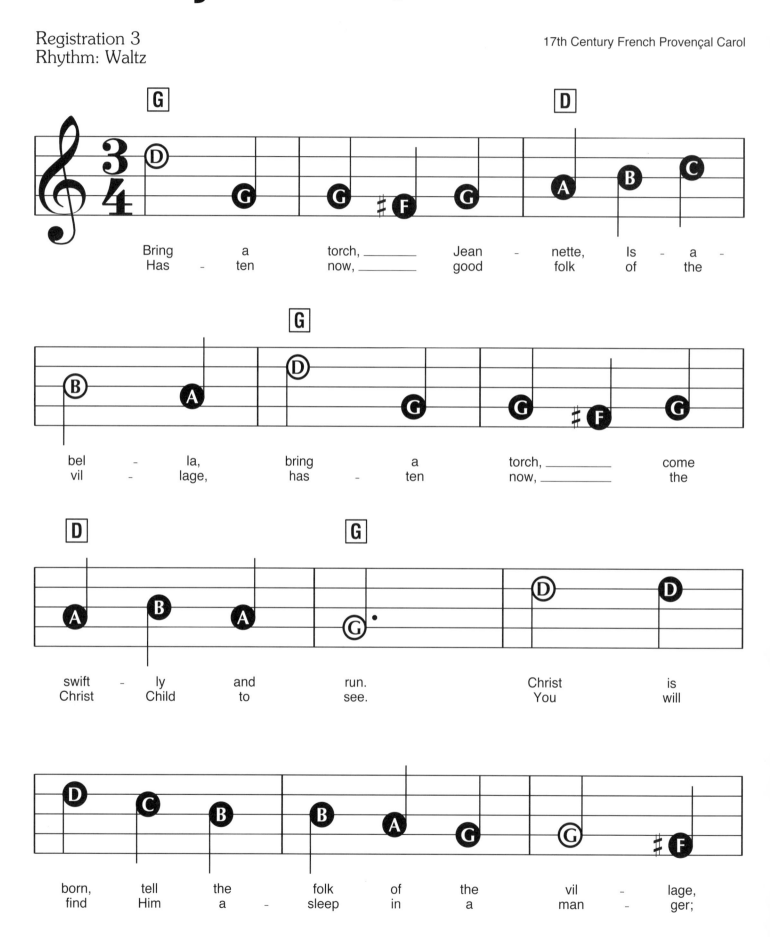

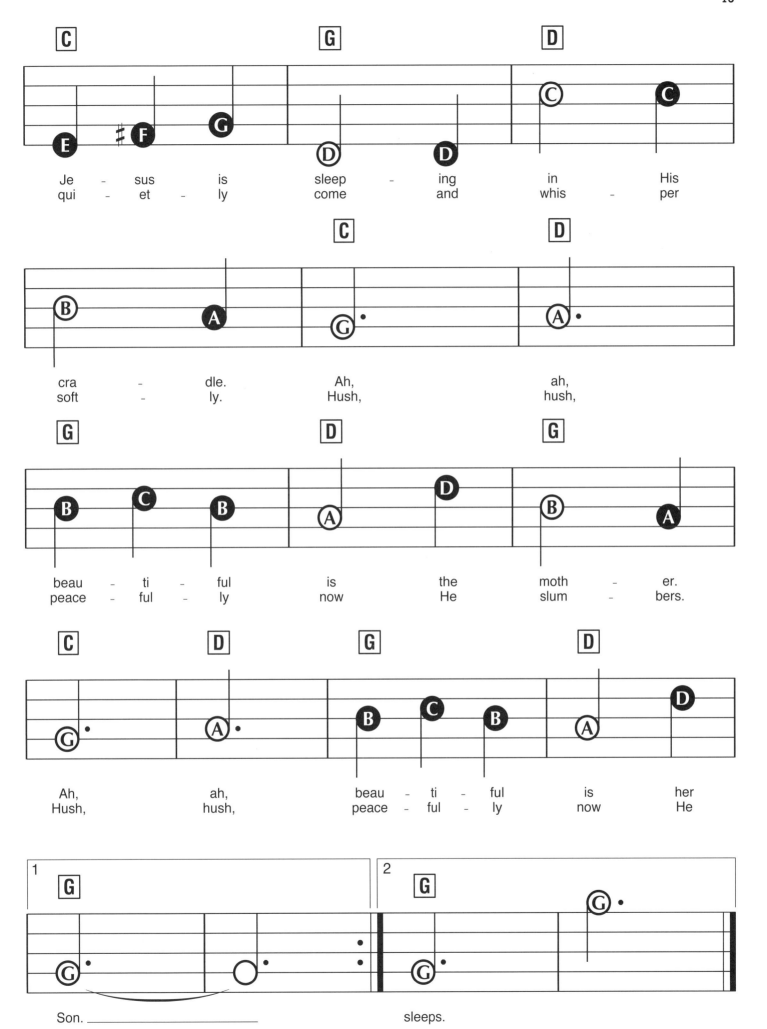

Christ Was Born on Christmas Day

Registration 6
Rhythm: None

Traditional

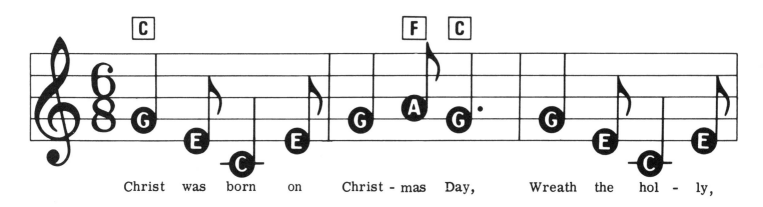

Christ was born on Christ - mas Day, Wreath the hol - ly,

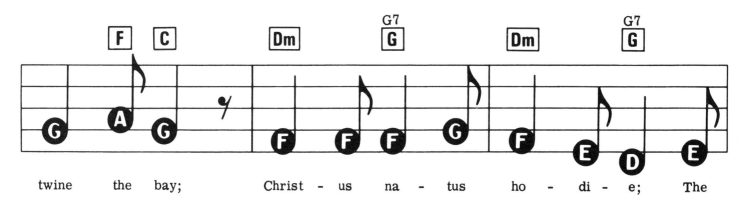

twine the bay; Christ - us na - tus ho - di - e; The

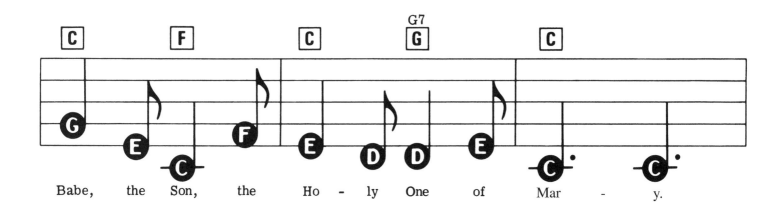

Babe, the Son, the Ho - ly One of Mar - y.

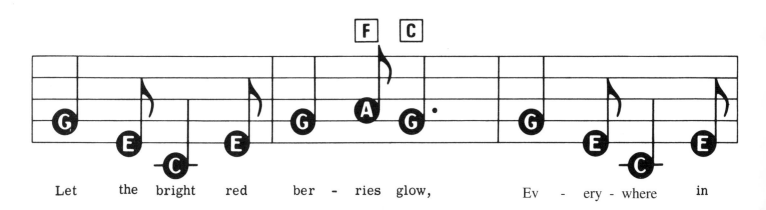

Let the bright red ber - ries glow, Ev - ery - where in

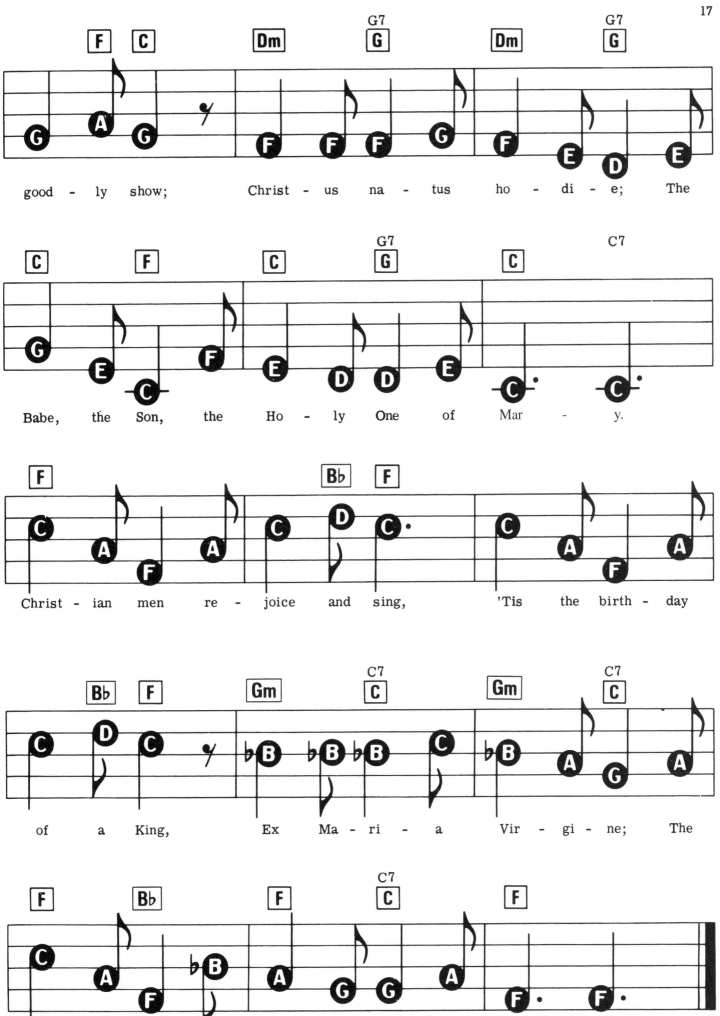

Coventry Carol

Registration 1
Rhythm: None

Words by Robert Croo
Traditional English Melody

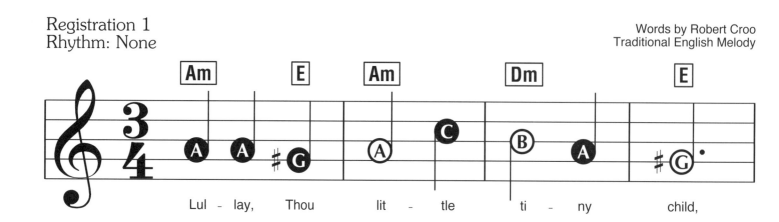

Lul - lay, Thou lit - tle ti - ny child,

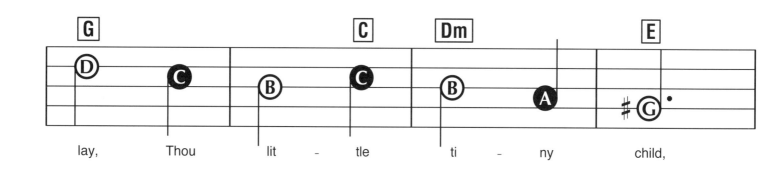

bye - bye, lul - ly, lul - lay. _____ Lul -

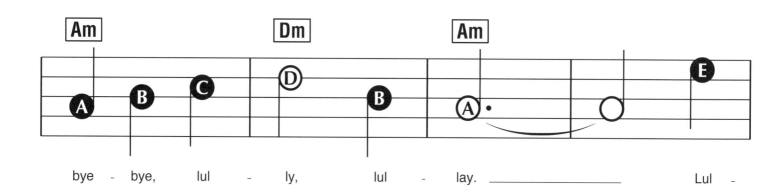

lay, Thou lit - tle ti - ny child,

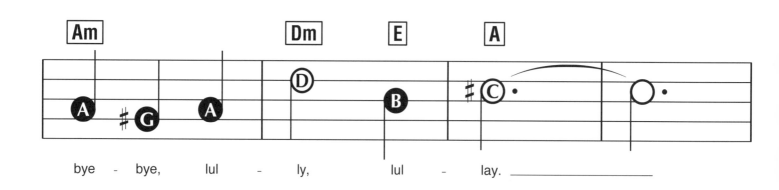

bye - bye, lul - ly, lul - lay. _____

19

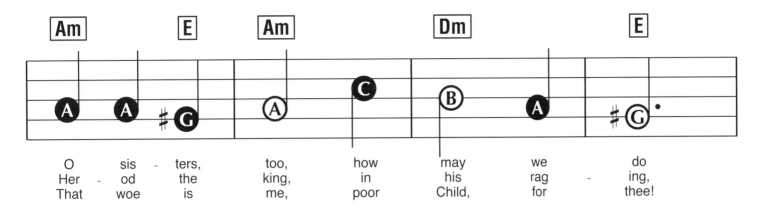

O sis - ters, too, how may we do
Her - od the king, in his rag - ing,
That woe is me, poor Child, for thee!

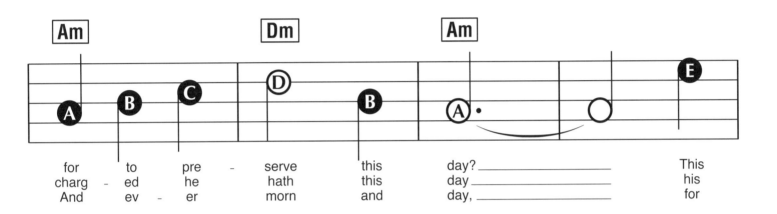

for to pre - serve this day? _____ This
charg - ed he hath this day _____ his
And ev - er morn and day, _____ for

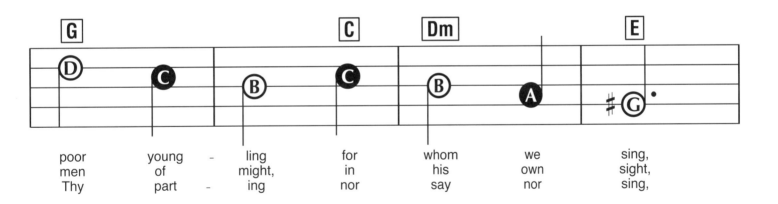

poor young - ling might, for whom we sing,
men of part - ing, in his own nor sight,
Thy part - ing, nor say nor sing,

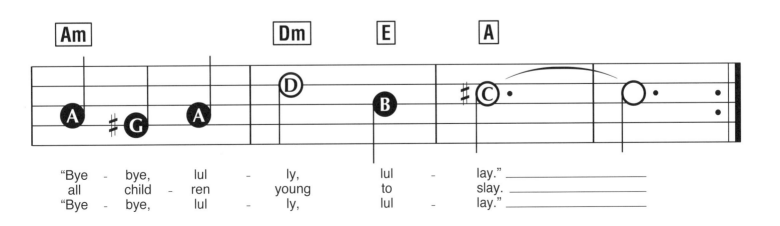

"Bye - bye, lul - ly, lul - lay." _____
all child - ren young to slay. _____
"Bye - bye, lul - ly, lul - lay." _____

Deck the Hall

Registration 7
Rhythm: Fox Trot

Traditional Welsh Carol

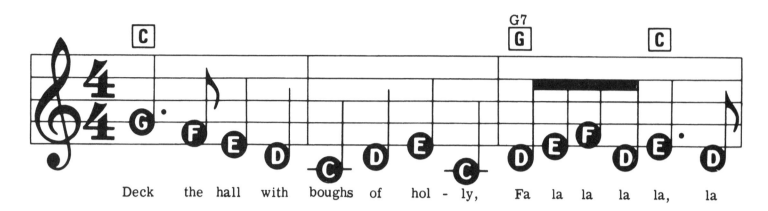

Deck the hall with boughs of hol - ly, Fa la la la la, la

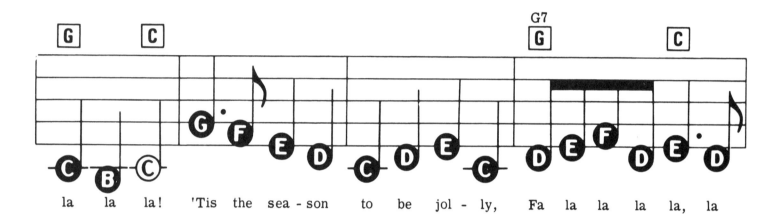

la la la! 'Tis the sea - son to be jol - ly, Fa la la la la, la

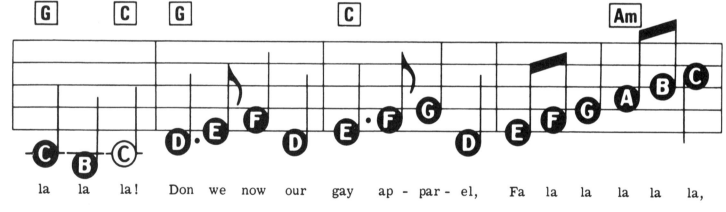

la la la! Don we now our gay ap - par - el, Fa la la la la la,

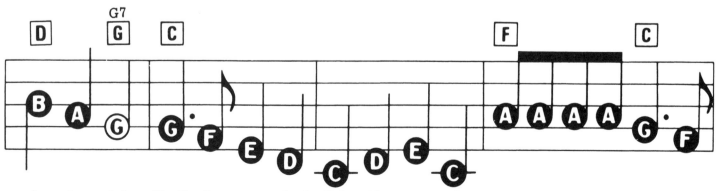

la la la! Troll the an - cient Yule-tide car - ol, Fa la la la la, la

21

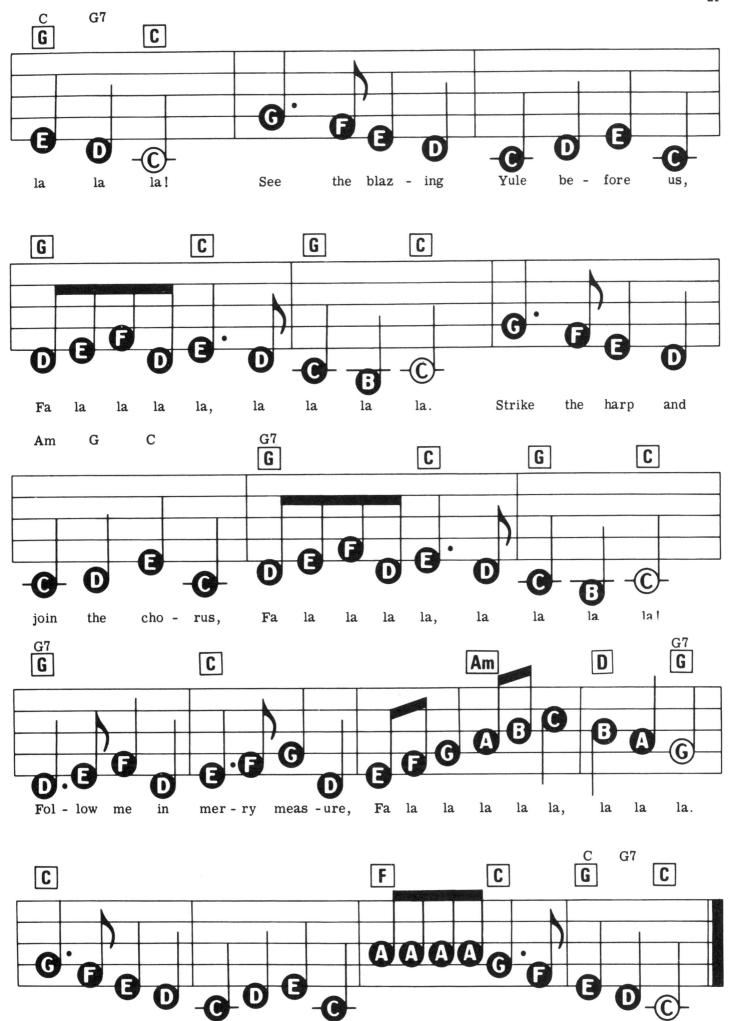

Ding Dong! Merrily on High!

Registration 5
Rhythm: March

French Carol

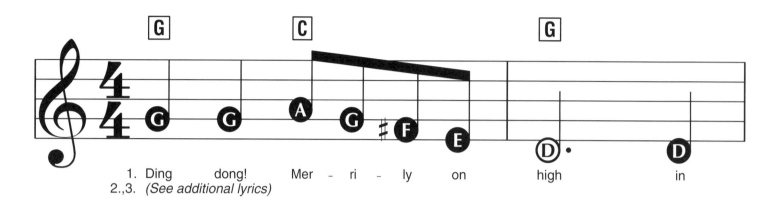

1. Ding dong! Mer – ri – ly on high in
2.,3. *(See additional lyrics)*

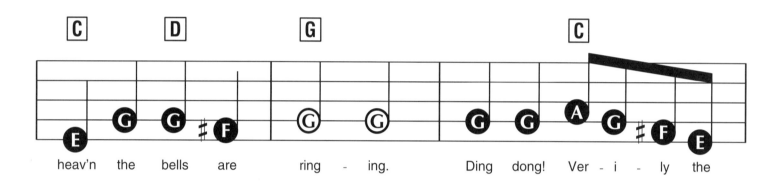

heav'n the bells are ring – ing. Ding dong! Ver – i – ly the

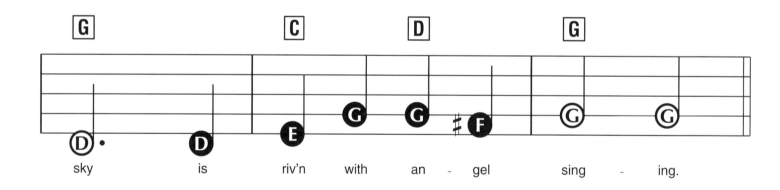

sky is riv'n with an – gel sing – ing.

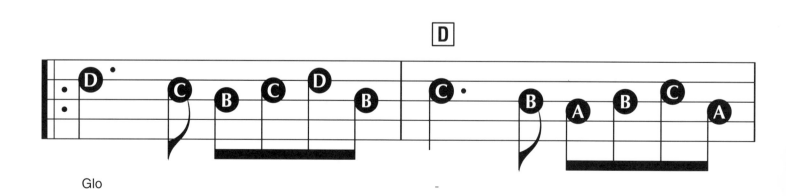

Glo

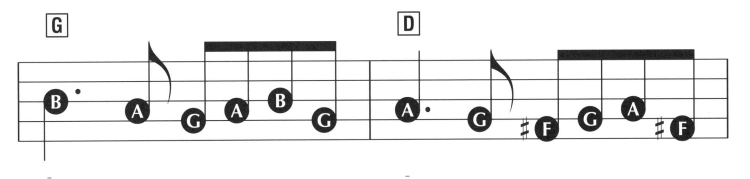

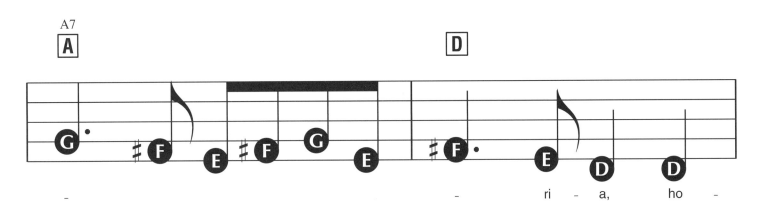

ri - a, ho -

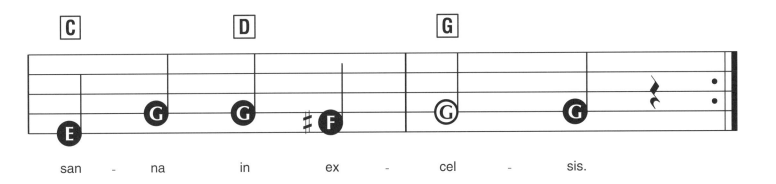

san - na in ex - cel - sis.

Additional Lyrics

2. E'en so here below, below,
   Let steeple bells be swungen,
   And io, io, io,
   By priest and people sungen.

   Gloria, hosanna in excelsis!
   Gloria, hosanna in excelsis!

3. Pray you, dutifully prime
   Your matin chime, ye ringers.
   May you beautifully rime
   Your evetime song, ye singers.

   Gloria, hosanna in excelsis!
   Gloria, hosanna in excelsis!

The First Noël

Registration 6
Rhythm: None

17th Century English Carol
Music from W. Sandys' *Christmas Carols*

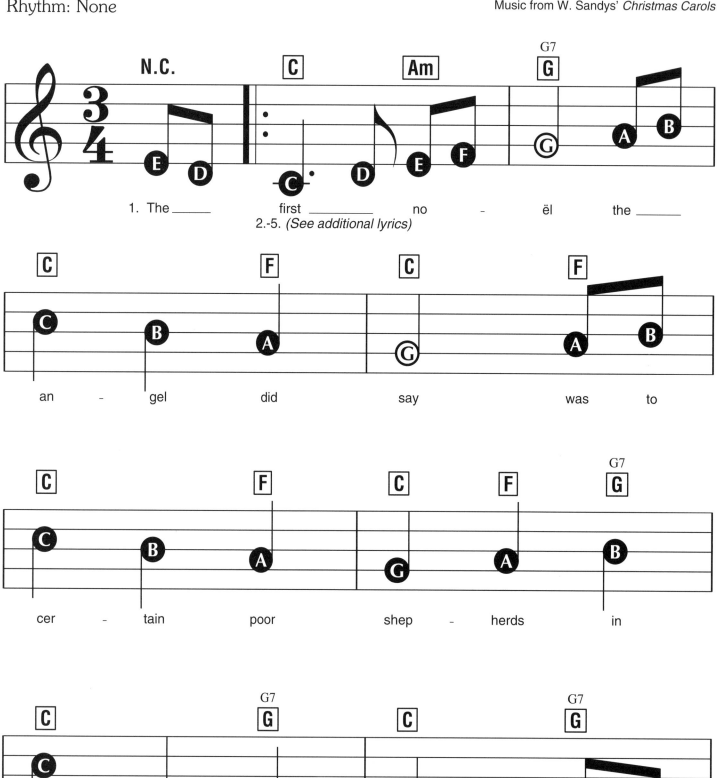

1. The _____ first _____ no - ël the _____
2.-5. *(See additional lyrics)*

an - gel did say was to

cer - tain poor shep - herds in

fields as they lay. In _____

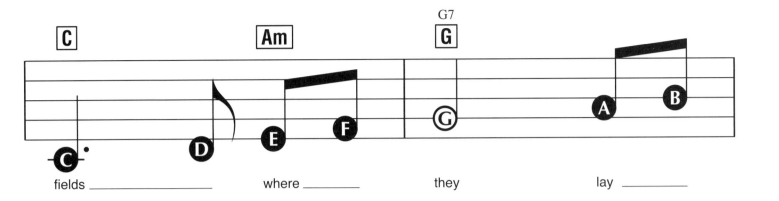

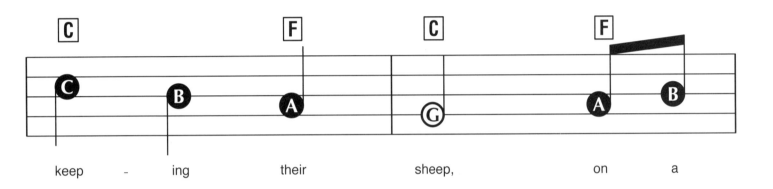

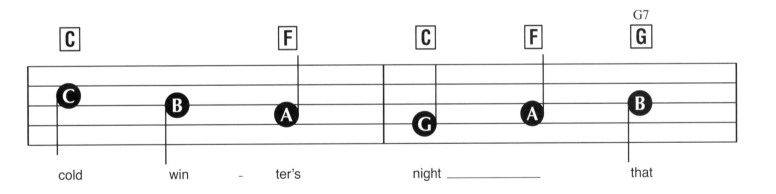

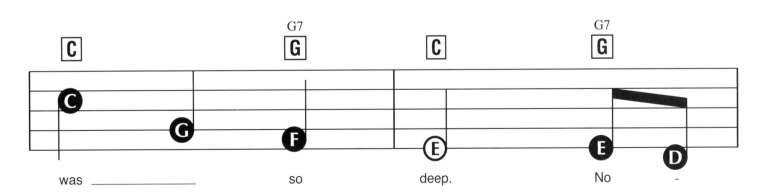

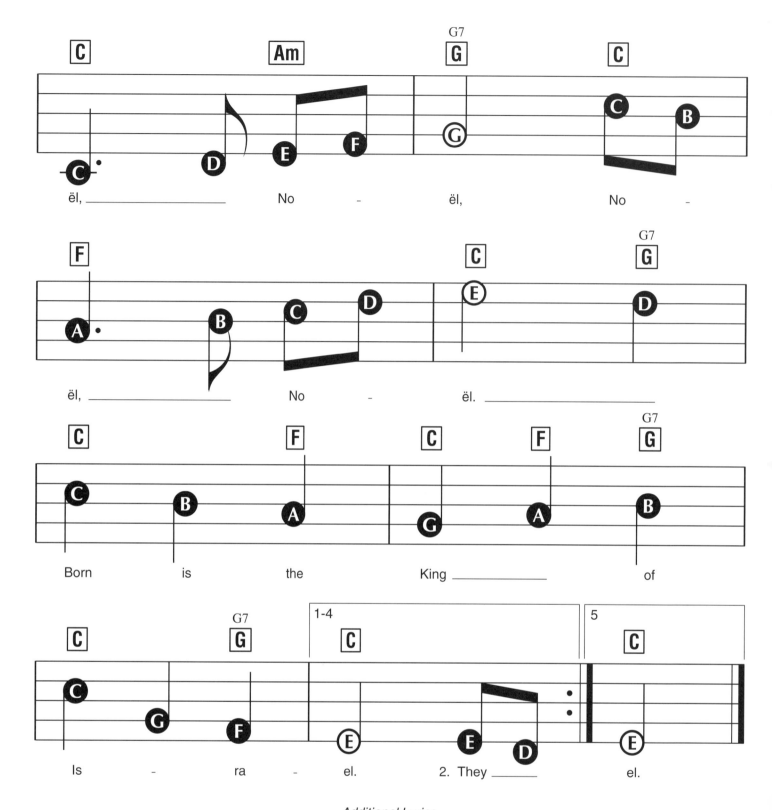

2. They looked up and saw a star
   Shining in the east beyond them far.
   And to the earth it gave great light,
   And so it continued both day and night.
   Noël, Noël, Noël, Noël.
   Born is the King of Israel.

3. And by the light of that same star
   Three wise men came from country far.
   To seek for a King was their intent,
   And to follow the star wherever it went.
   Noël, Noël, Noël, Noël.
   Born is the King of Israel.

4. This star drew nigh to the northwest,
   O'er Bethlehem it took its rest.
   And there it did both stop and stay
   Right over the place where Jesus lay.
   Noël, Noël, Noël, Noël.
   Born is the King of Israel.

5. Then entered in those wise men three
   Full reverently upon their knee.
   And offered there, in His presence,
   Their gold, and myrrh, and frankincense.
   Noël, Noël, Noël, Noël.
   Born is the King of Israel.

Go, Tell It on the Mountain

Registration 5
Rhythm: Swing

African-American Spiritual
Verses by John W. Work, Jr.

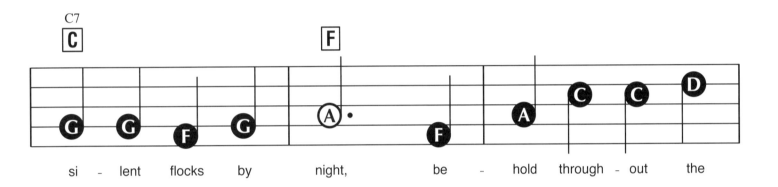

While shep - herds kept their watch - ing o'er

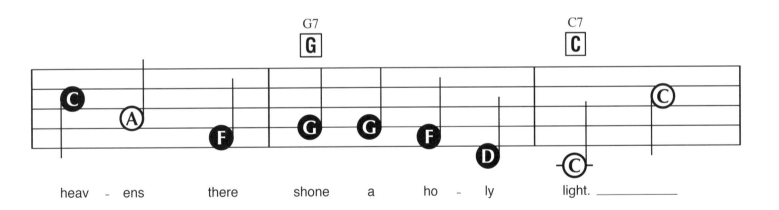

si - lent flocks by night, be - hold through - out the

heav - ens there shone a ho - ly light. _____

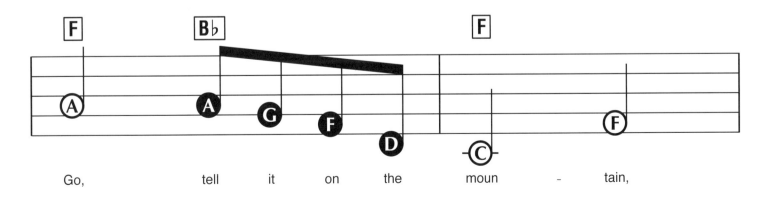

Go, tell it on the moun - tain,

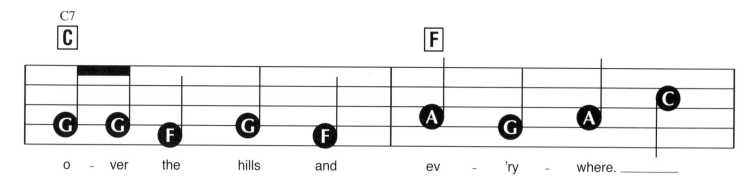

o - ver the hills and ev - 'ry - where. _____

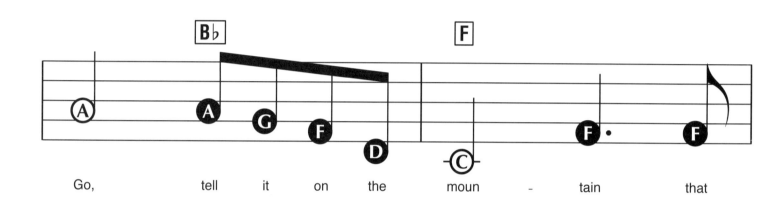

Go, tell it on the moun - tain that

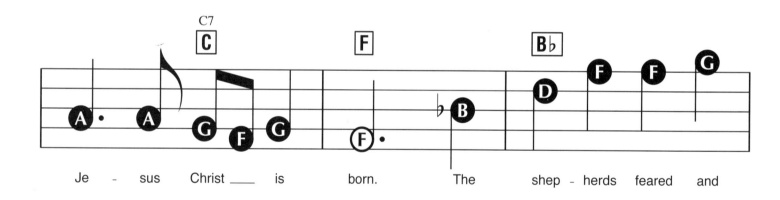

Je - sus Christ ___ is born. The shep - herds feared and

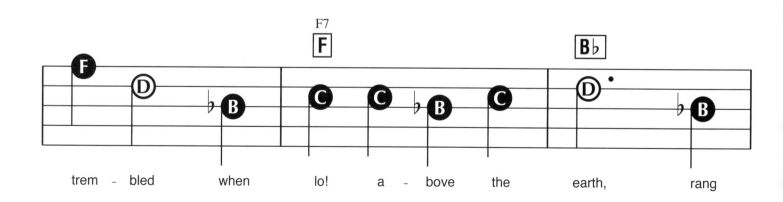

trem - bled when lo! a - bove the earth, rang

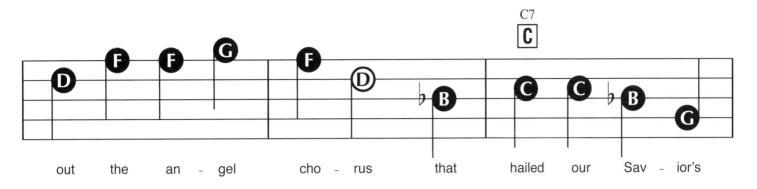

out the an - gel cho - rus that hailed our Sav - ior's

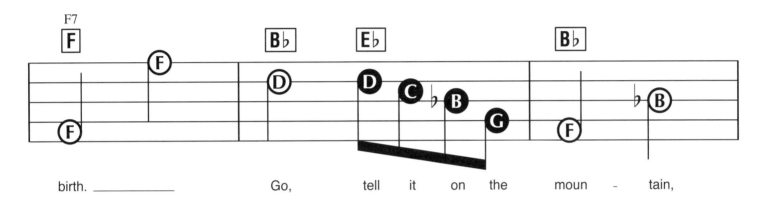

birth. _____ Go, tell it on the moun - tain,

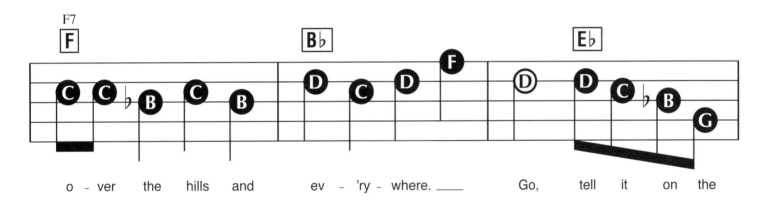

o - ver the hills and ev - 'ry - where. ___ Go, tell it on the

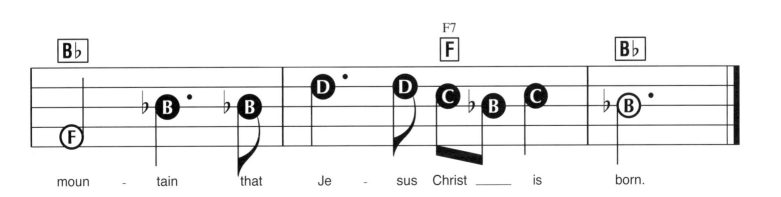

moun - tain that Je - sus Christ ___ is born.

The Friendly Beasts

Registration 2
Rhythm: Waltz

Traditional English Carol

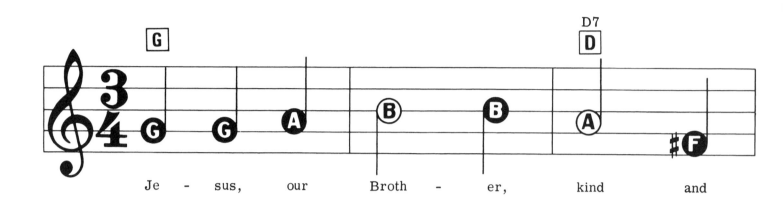

Je - sus, our Broth - er, kind and

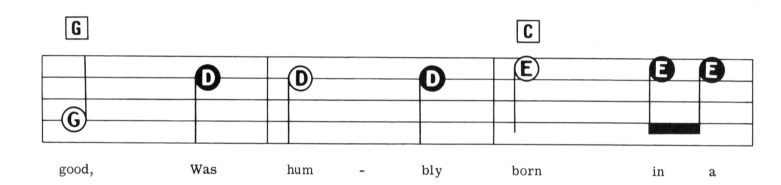

good, Was hum - bly born in a

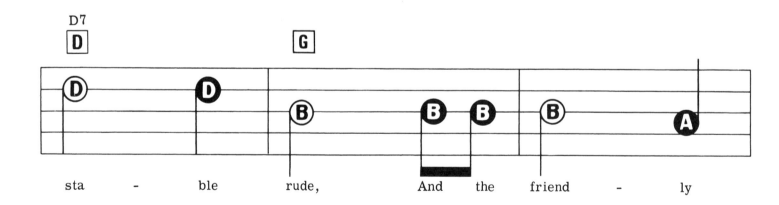

sta - ble rude, And the friend - ly

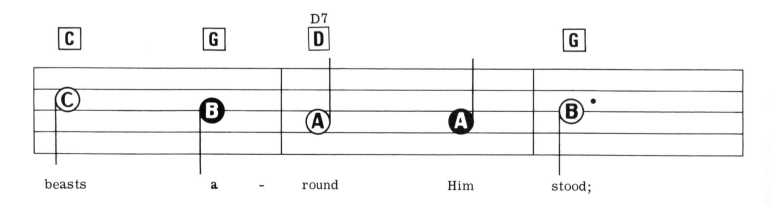

beasts a - round Him stood;

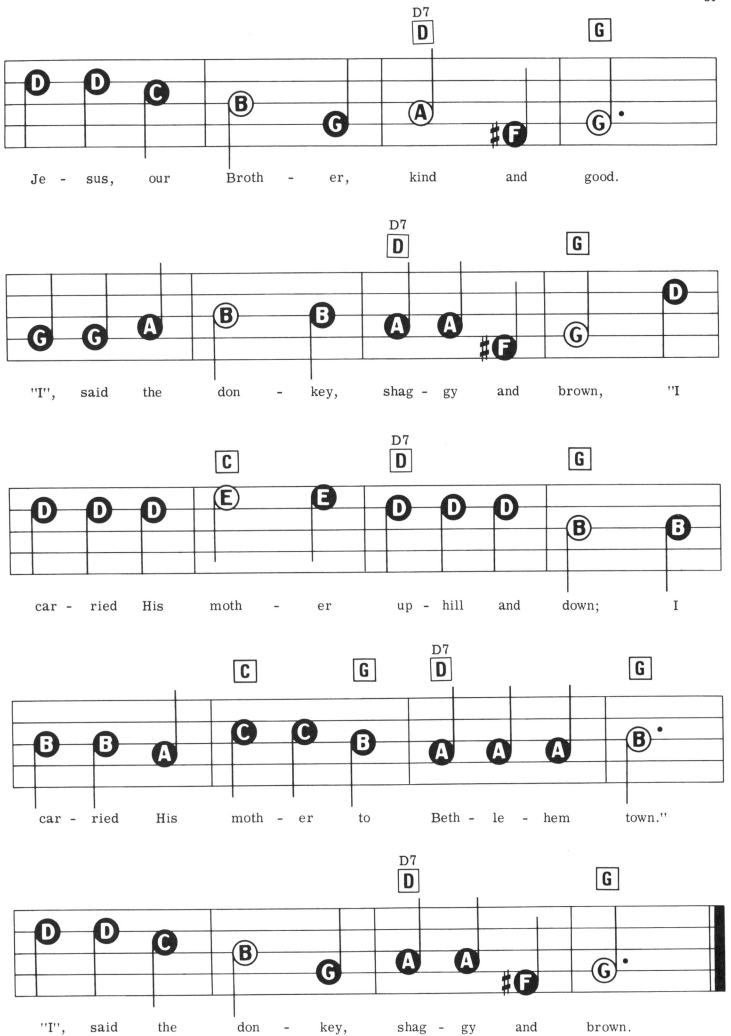

God Rest Ye Merry, Gentlemen

Registration 6
Rhythm: None

Traditional English Carol

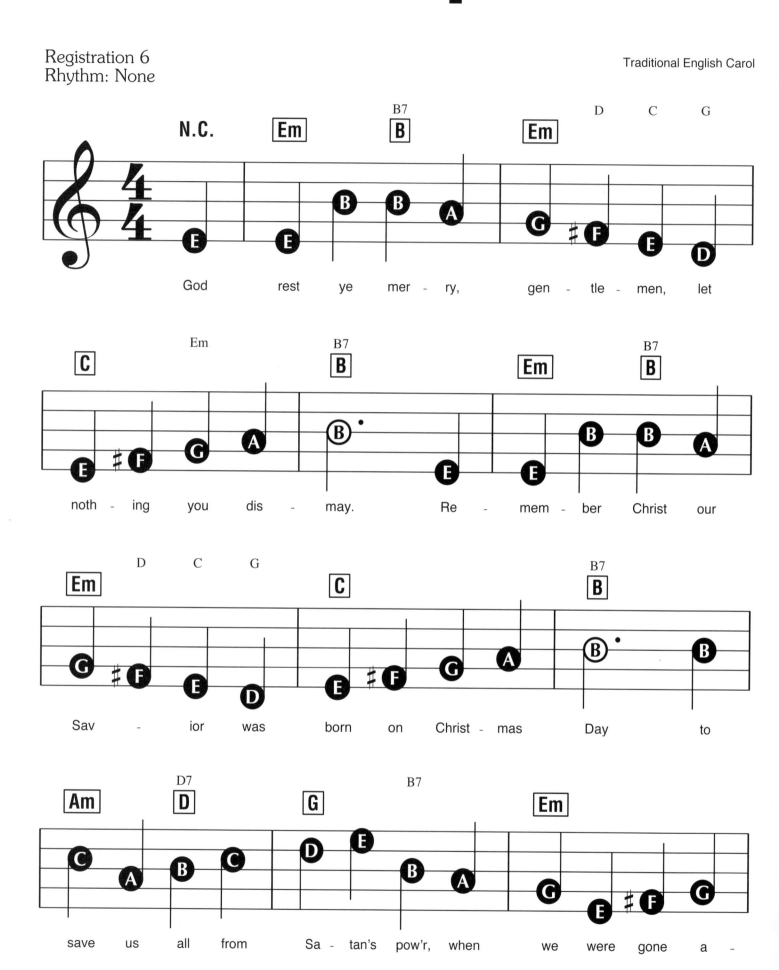

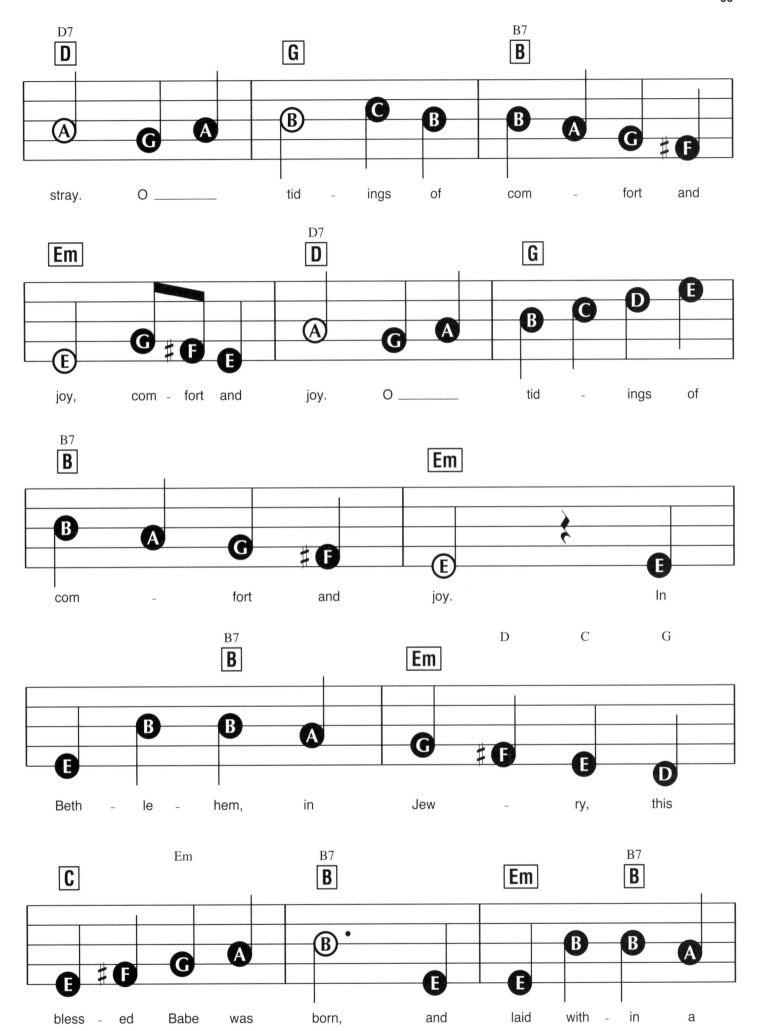

34

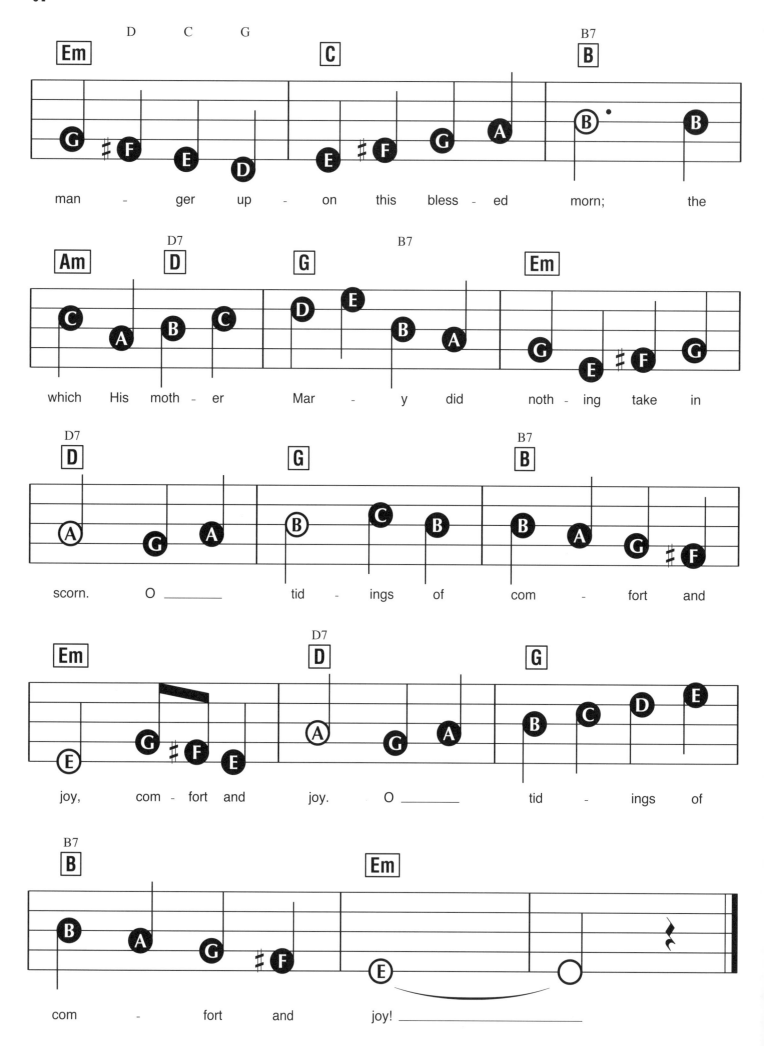

Good King Wenceslas

Registration 4
Rhythm: March

Words by John M. Neale
Music from *Piae Cantiones*

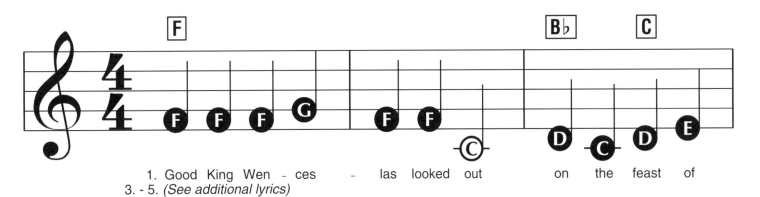

1. Good King Wen - ces - las looked out on the feast of
3. - 5. *(See additional lyrics)*

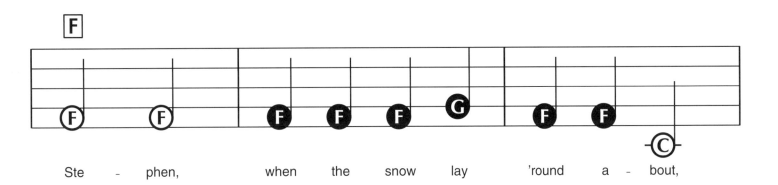

Ste - phen, when the snow lay 'round a - bout,

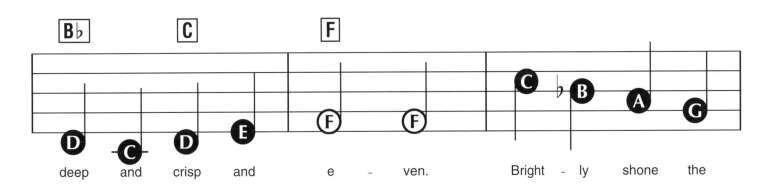

deep and crisp and e - ven. Bright - ly shone the

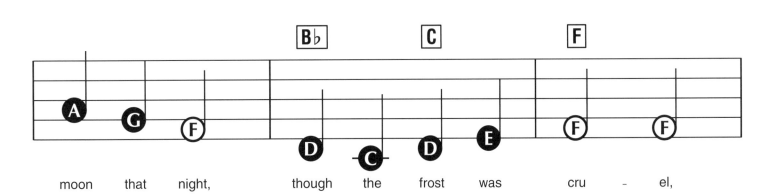

moon that night, though the frost was cru - el,

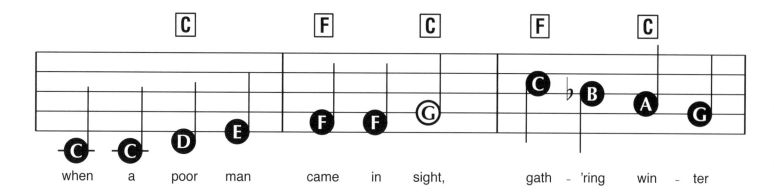

when a poor man came in sight, gath - 'ring win - ter

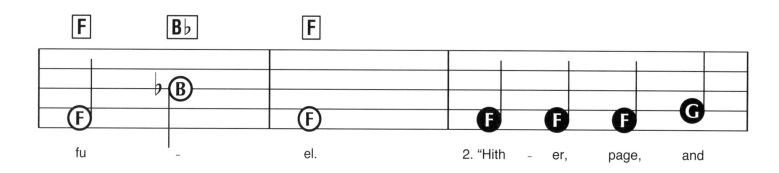

fu - el. 2. "Hith - er, page, and

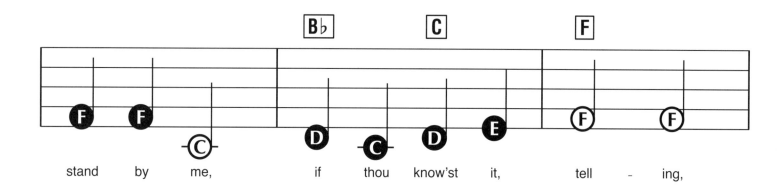

stand by me, if thou know'st it, tell - ing,

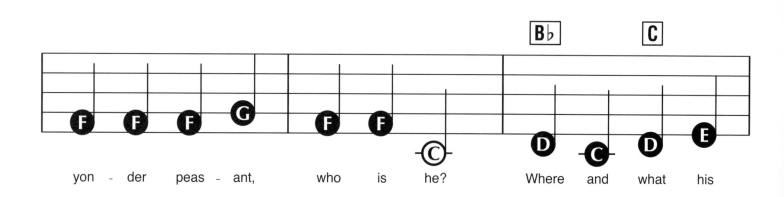

yon - der peas - ant, who is he? Where and what his

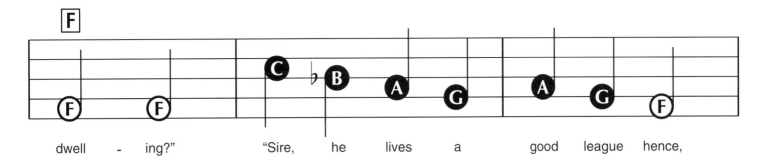

dwell - ing?" "Sire, he lives a good league hence,

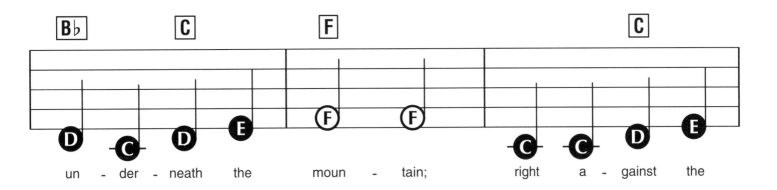

un - der - neath the moun - tain; right a - gainst the

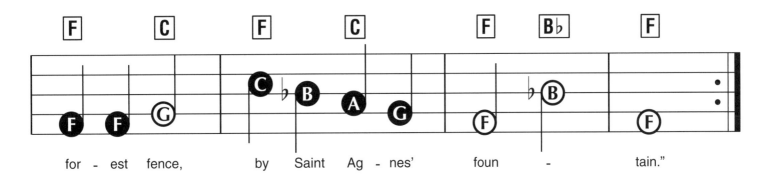

for - est fence, by Saint Ag - nes' foun - tain."

Additional Lyrics

3. "Bring me flesh, and bring me wine,
Bring me pine logs hither.
Thou and I will see him dine
When we bear them thither."
Page and monarch forth they went,
Forth they went together,
Through the rude wind's wild lament
And the bitter weather.

4. "Sire, the night is darker now,
And the wind blows stronger.
Fails my heart, I know not how,
I can go no longer."
"Mark my footsteps, my good page,
Tread thou in them boldly.
Thou shalt find the winter's rage
Freeze thy blood less coldly."

5. In his master's steps he trod,
Where the snow lay dinted;
Heat was in the very sod
Which the saint had printed.
Therefore, Christian men, be sure,
Wealth or rank possessing,
Ye who now will bless the poor
Shall yourselves find blessing.

Good Christian Men, Rejoice

Registration 6
Rhythm: None

14th Century Latin Text
Translated by John Mason Neale
14th Century German Melody

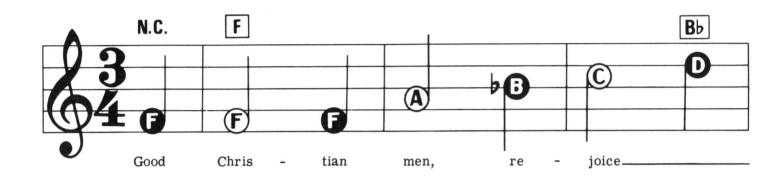

Good Chris - tian men, re - joice_____

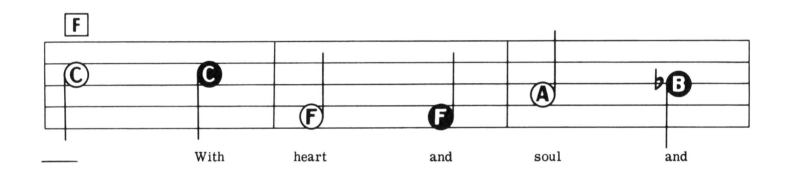

_____ With heart and soul and

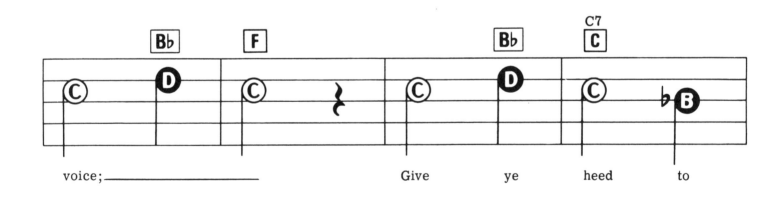

voice;_____ Give ye heed to

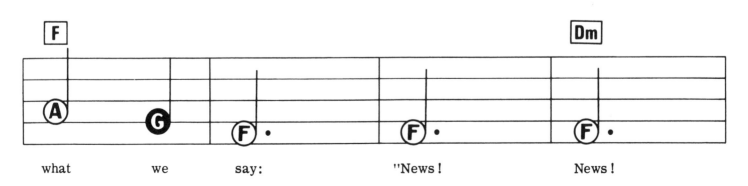

what we say: "News! News!

39

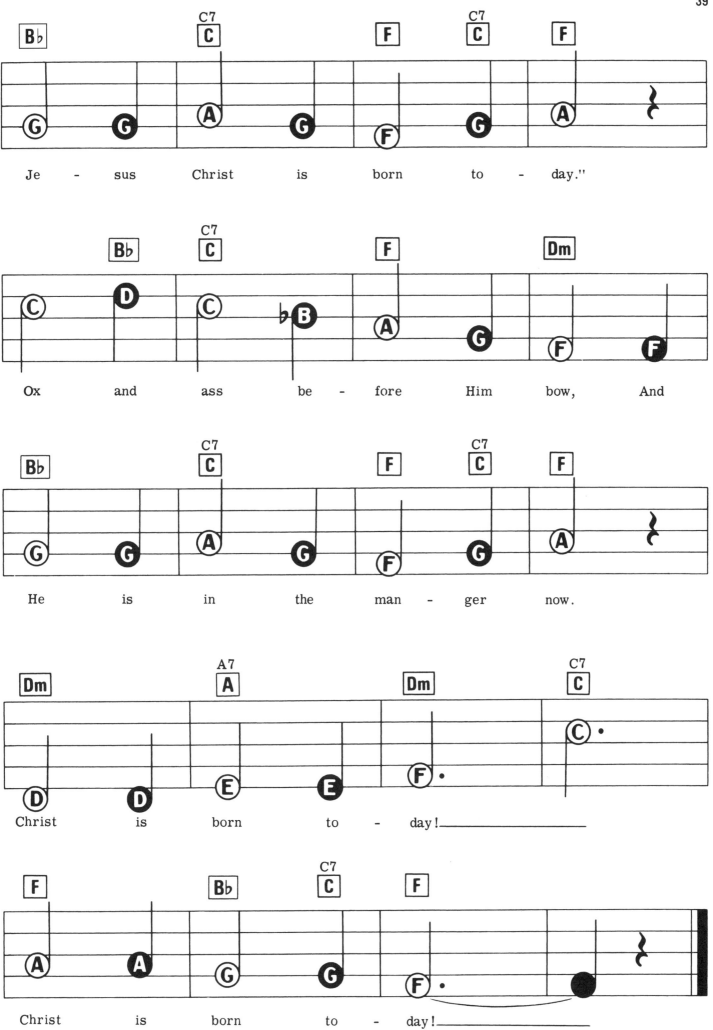

Hark! The Herald Angels Sing

Words by Charles Wesley
Music by Felix Mendelssohn-Bartholdy
Adapted by William H. Cummings

Registration 6
Rhythm: None

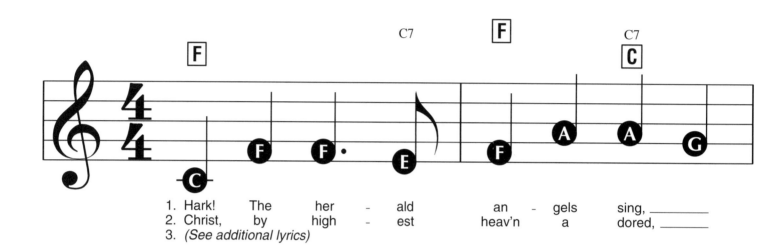

1. Hark! The her - ald an - gels sing, _____
2. Christ, by high - est heav'n a - dored, _____
3. *(See additional lyrics)*

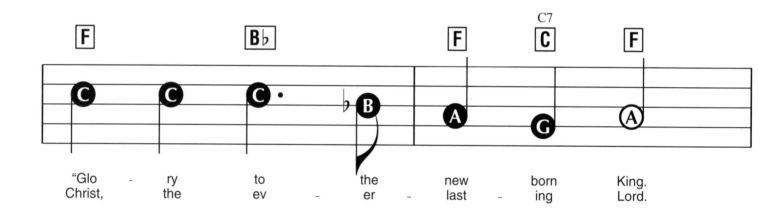

"Glo - ry to the new born King.
Christ, the ev - er - last - ing Lord.

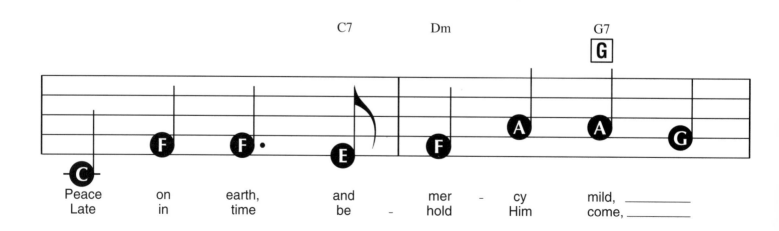

Peace on earth, and mer - cy mild, _____
Late in time be - hold Him come, _____

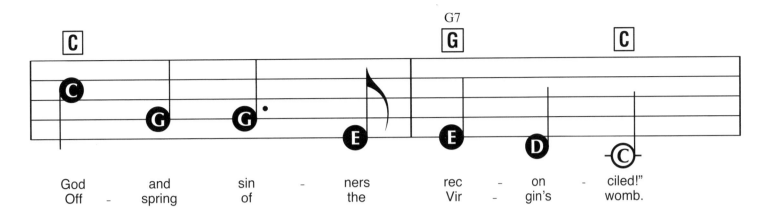

God   and   sin -   ners   rec - on - ciled!"
Off - spring of   the   Vir - gin's   womb.

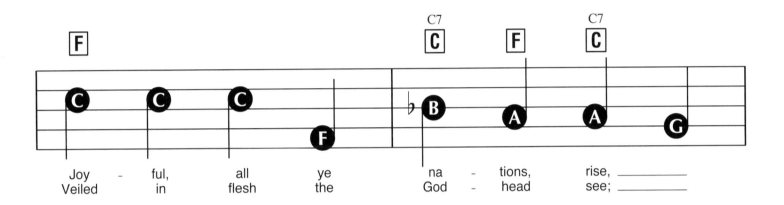

Joy - ful,   all   ye   na - tions,   rise, _____
Veiled in   flesh   the   God - head   see; _____

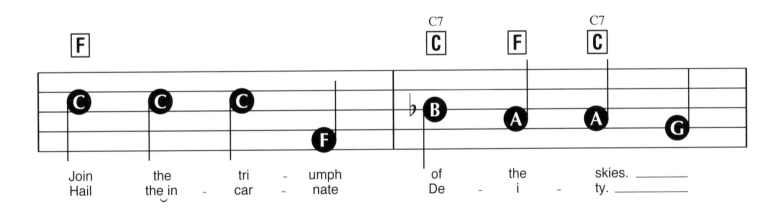

Join   the   tri - umph   of   the   skies. _____
Hail   the in - car - nate   De - i - ty. _____

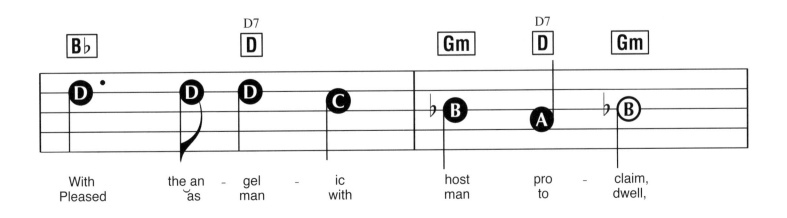

With   the an - gel - ic with   host   pro - claim,
Pleased as   man   with   man   to   dwell,

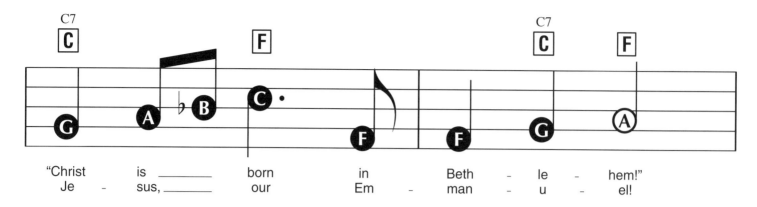

"Christ is _____ born in Beth - le - hem!"
Je - sus, _____ our Em - man - u - el!

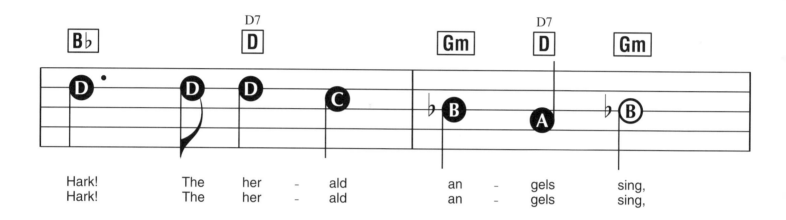

Hark! The her - ald an - gels sing,
Hark! The her - ald an - gels sing,

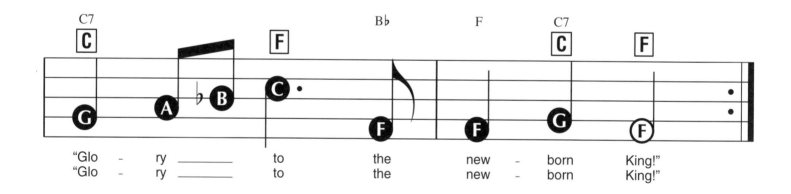

"Glo - ry _____ to the new - born King!"
"Glo - ry _____ to the new new - born King!"

Additional Lyrics

3. Hail the heaven-born Prince of Peace!
   Hail the Sun of Righteousness!
   Light and life to all he brings,
   Risen with healing in His wings.
   Mild He lays His glory by,
   Born that man no more may die.
   Born to raise the sons of earth,
   Born to give them second birth.

   Hark! the herald angels sing,
   "Glory to the newborn King!"

Jingle Bells

Registration 7
Rhythm: Fox Trot or Swing

Words and Music by
J. Pierpont

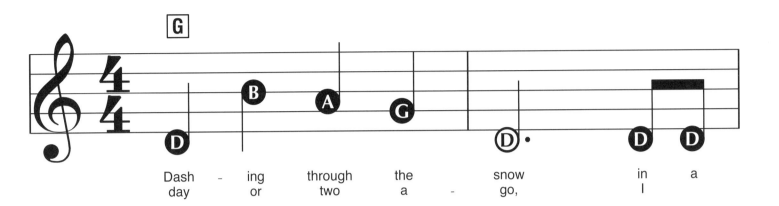

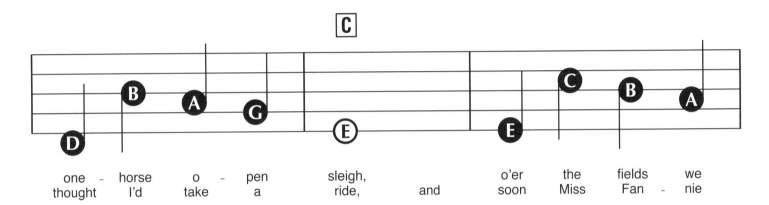

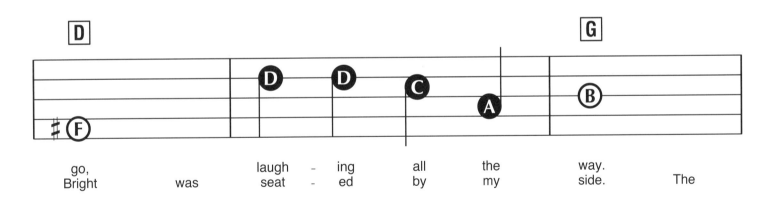

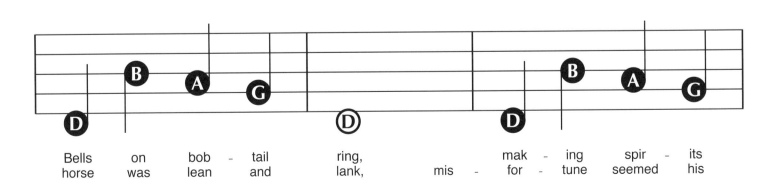

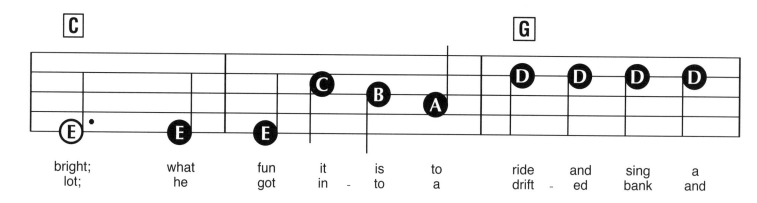

bright;   what   fun   it   is   to   ride   and   sing   a
lot;   he   got   in - to   a   drift - ed   bank   and

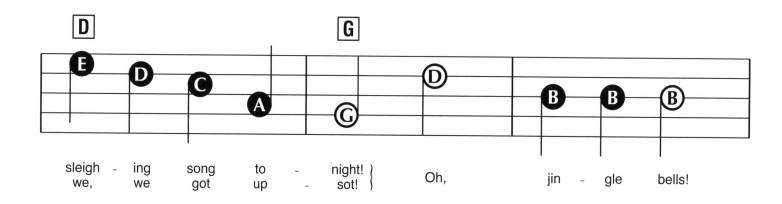

sleigh - ing   song   to - night! }   Oh,   jin - gle   bells!
we,   we   got   up - sot! }

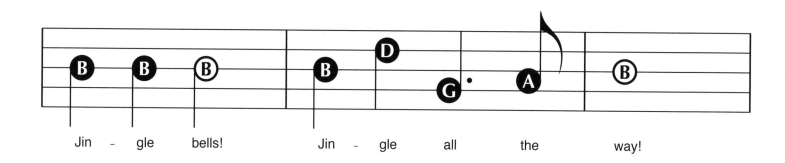

Jin - gle   bells!   Jin - gle   all   the   way!

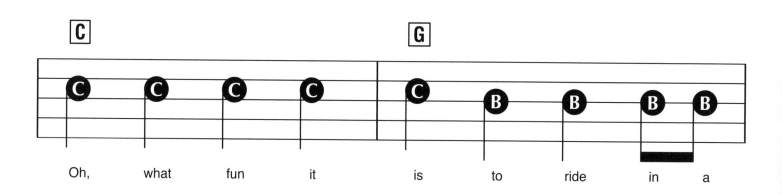

Oh,   what   fun   it   is   to   ride   in   a

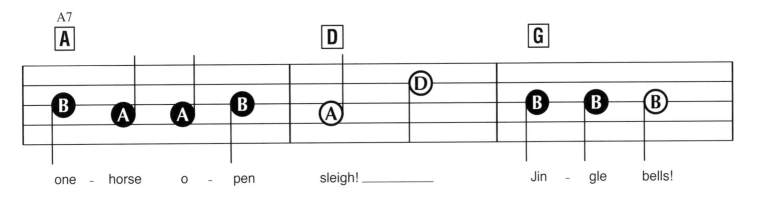

one - horse o - pen sleigh! _____ Jin - gle bells!

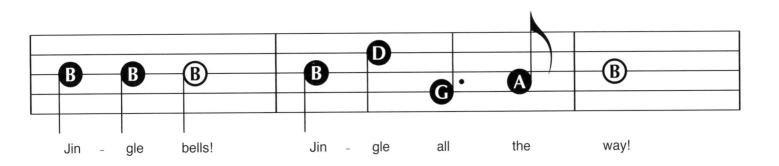

Jin - gle bells! Jin - gle all the way!

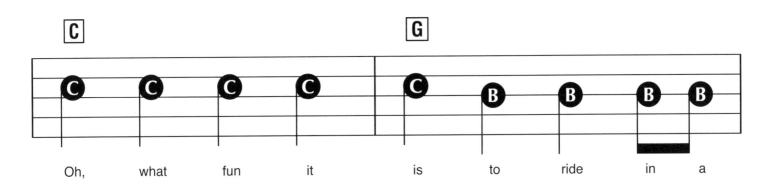

Oh, what fun it is to ride in a

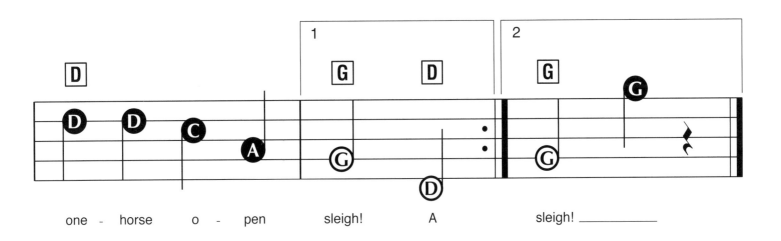

one - horse o - pen sleigh! A sleigh! _____

Here We Come A-Wassailing

Registration 3
Rhythm: 6/8 March

Traditional

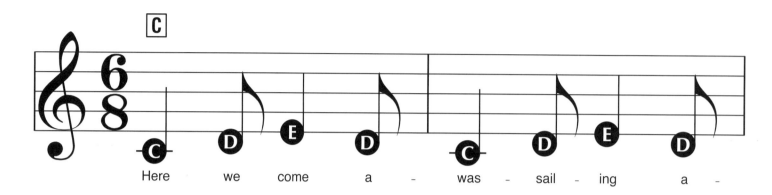

Here   we   come   a –   was - sail - ing   a -

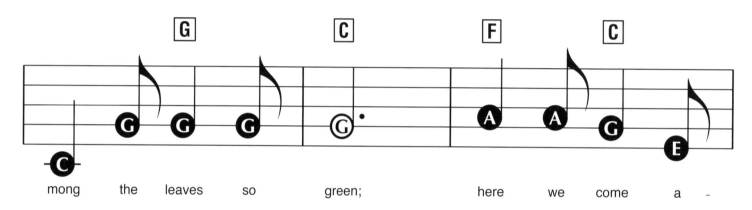

mong   the   leaves   so   green;   here   we   come   a -

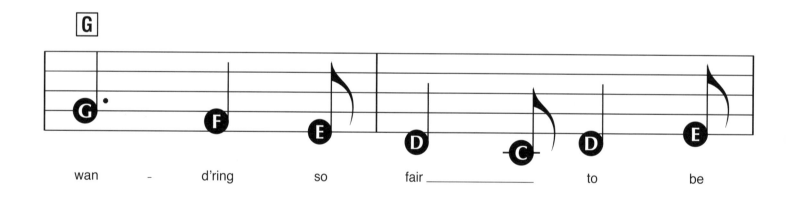

wan – d'ring   so   fair _____   to   be

Rhythm: Fox Trot

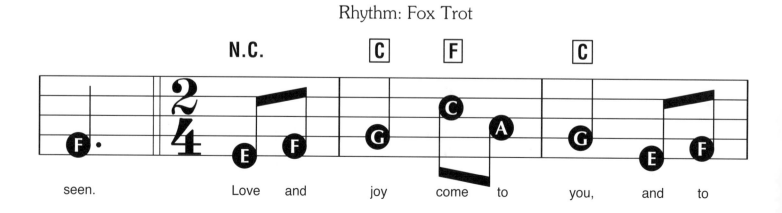

seen.   Love   and   joy   come   to   you,   and   to

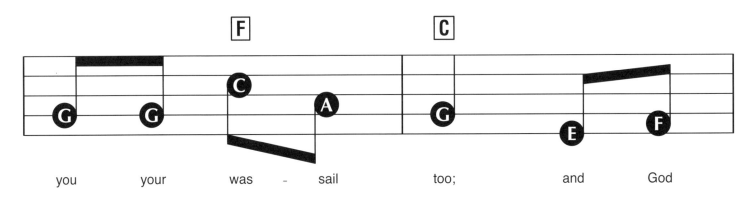

you your was - sail too; and God

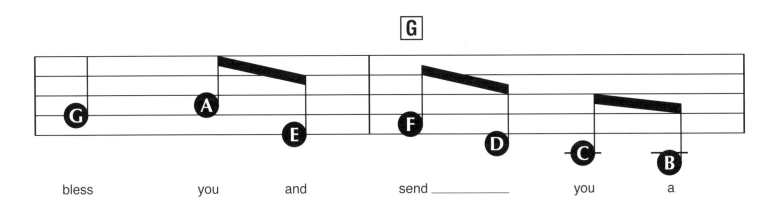

bless you and send _____ you a

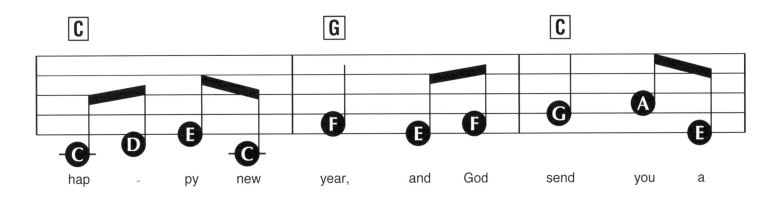

hap - py new year, and God send you a

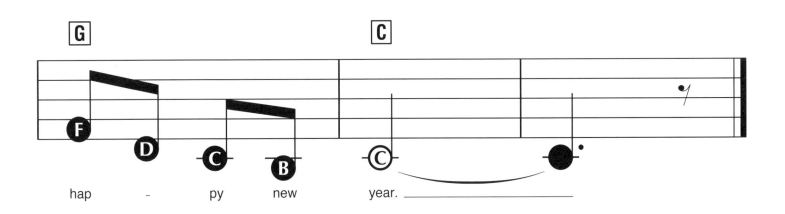

hap - py new year. _____

I Heard the Bells on Christmas Day

Registration 7
Rhythm: Ballad or Fox Trot

Words by Henry Wadsworth Longfellow
Music by John Baptiste Calkin

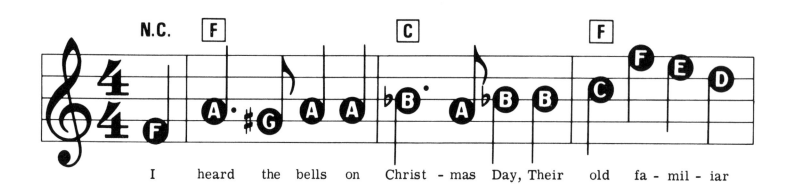

I heard the bells on Christ - mas Day, Their old fa - mil - iar

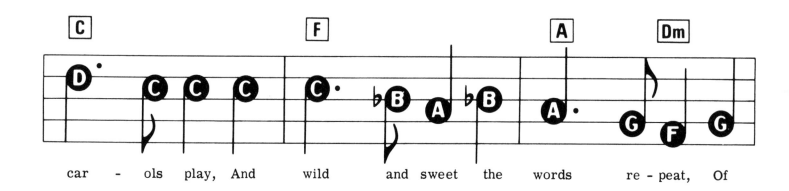

car - ols play, And wild and sweet the words re - peat, Of

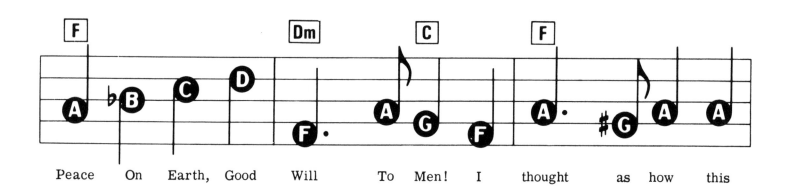

Peace On Earth, Good Will To Men! I thought as how this

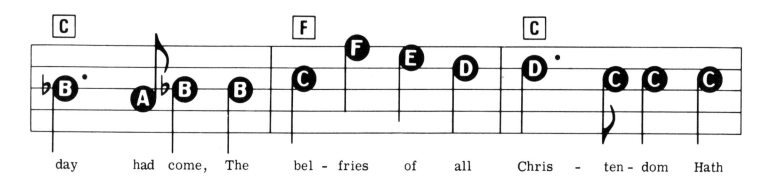

day had come, The bel - fries of all Chris - ten - dom Hath

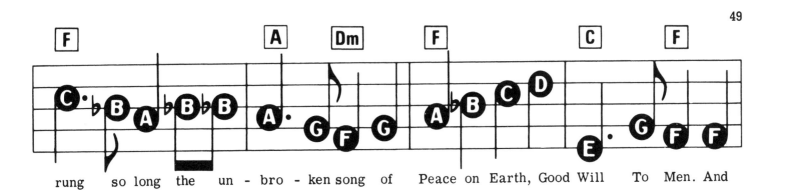
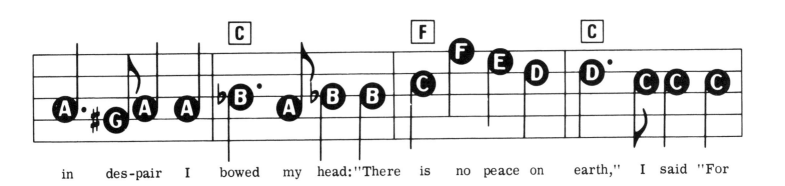

rung so long the un - bro - ken song of Peace on Earth, Good Will To Men. And

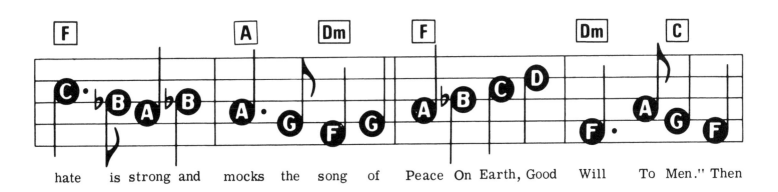

in des-pair I bowed my head:"There is no peace on earth," I said "For

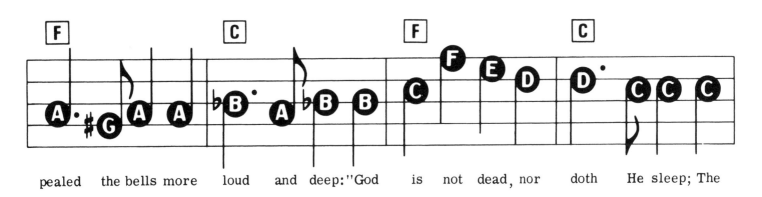

hate is strong and mocks the song of Peace On Earth, Good Will To Men." Then

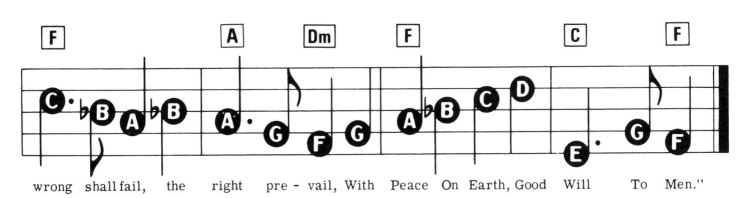

pealed the bells more loud and deep:"God is not dead, nor doth He sleep; The

wrong shall fail, the right pre - vail, With Peace On Earth, Good Will To Men."

I Saw Three Ships

Registration 8
Rhythm: 6/8 March or None

Traditional English Carol

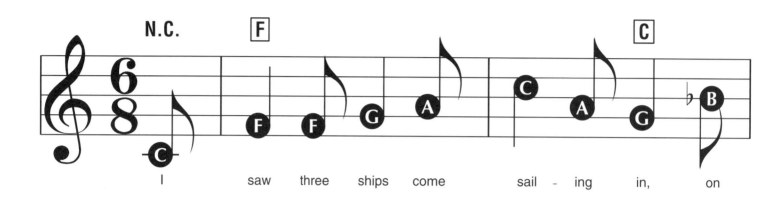

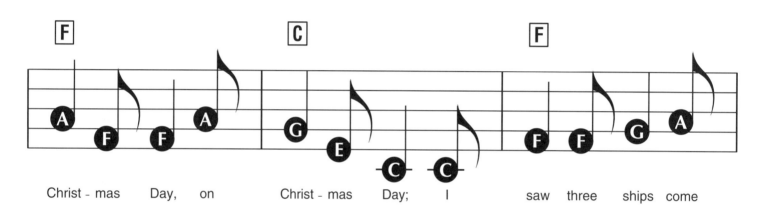

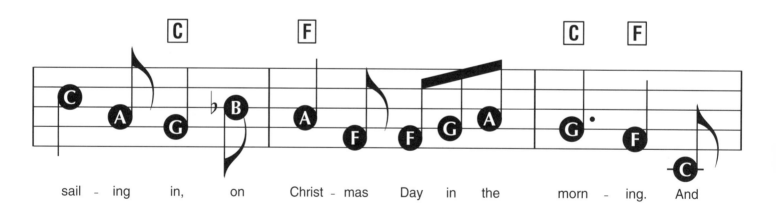

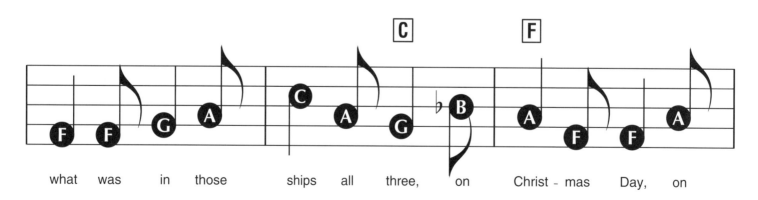

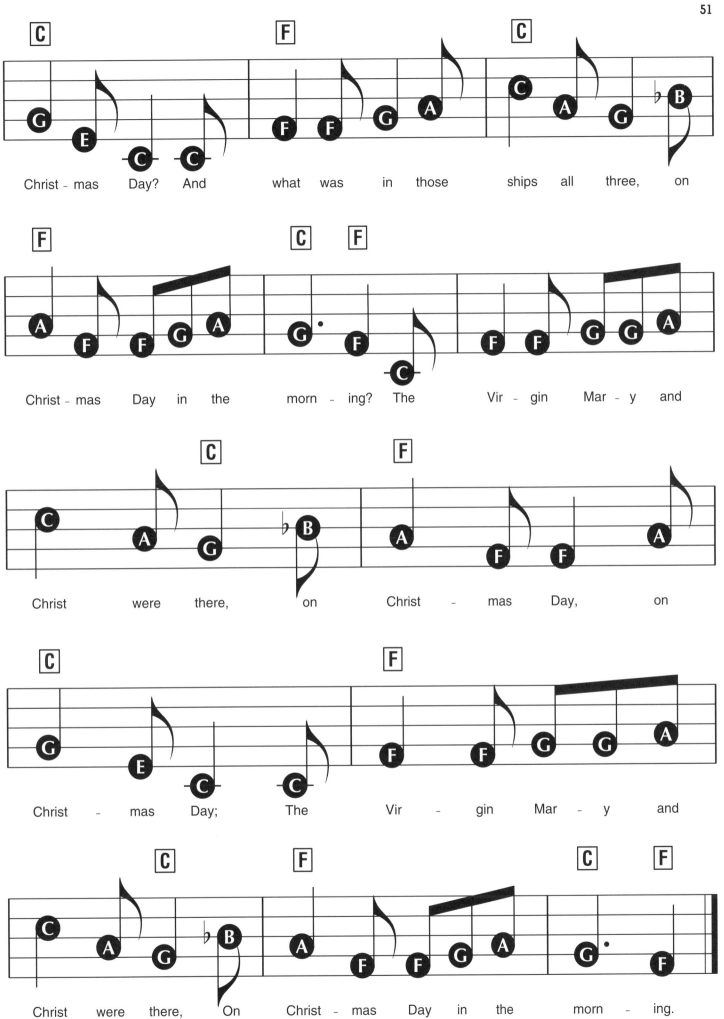

It Came Upon the Midnight Clear

Registration 6
Rhythm: None

Words by Edmund Hamilton Sears
Music by Richard Storrs Willis

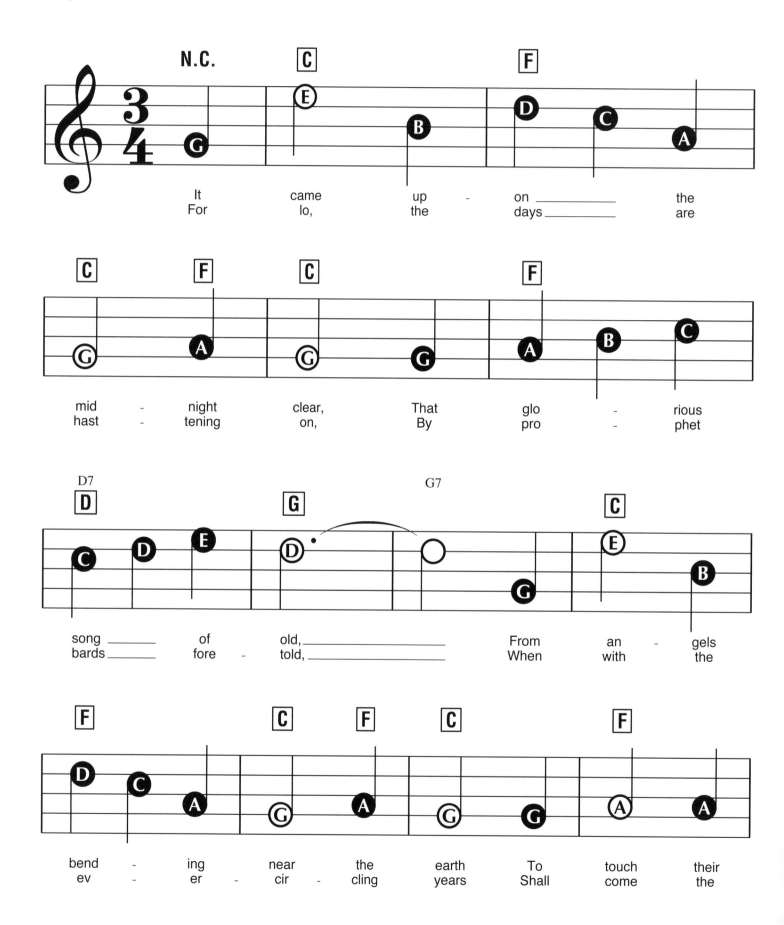

53

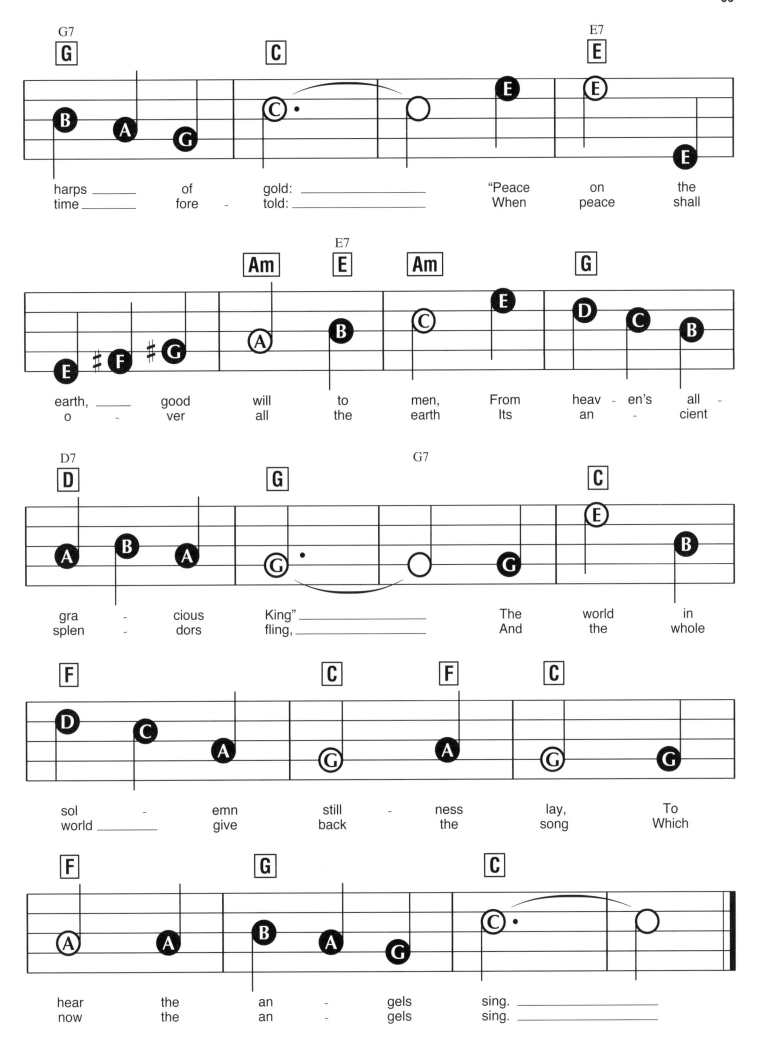

Jolly Old St. Nicholas

Registration 2
Rhythm: Fox Trot or Swing

Traditional 19th Century American Carol

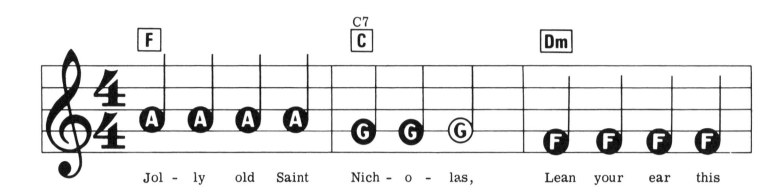

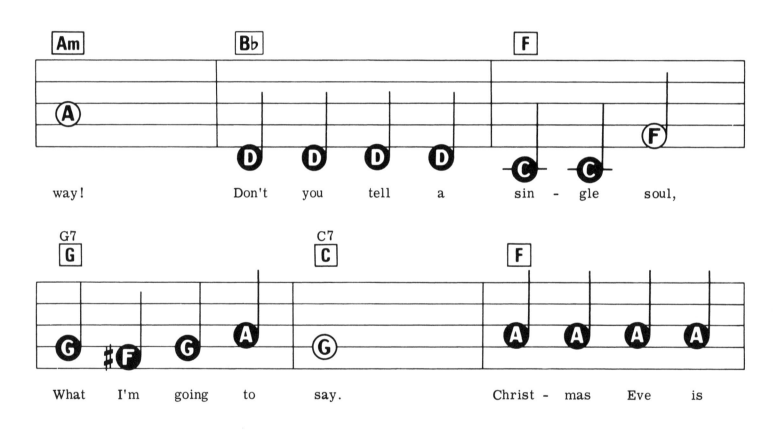

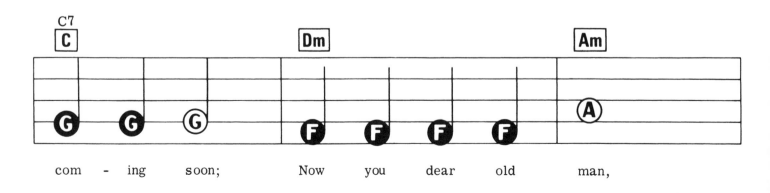

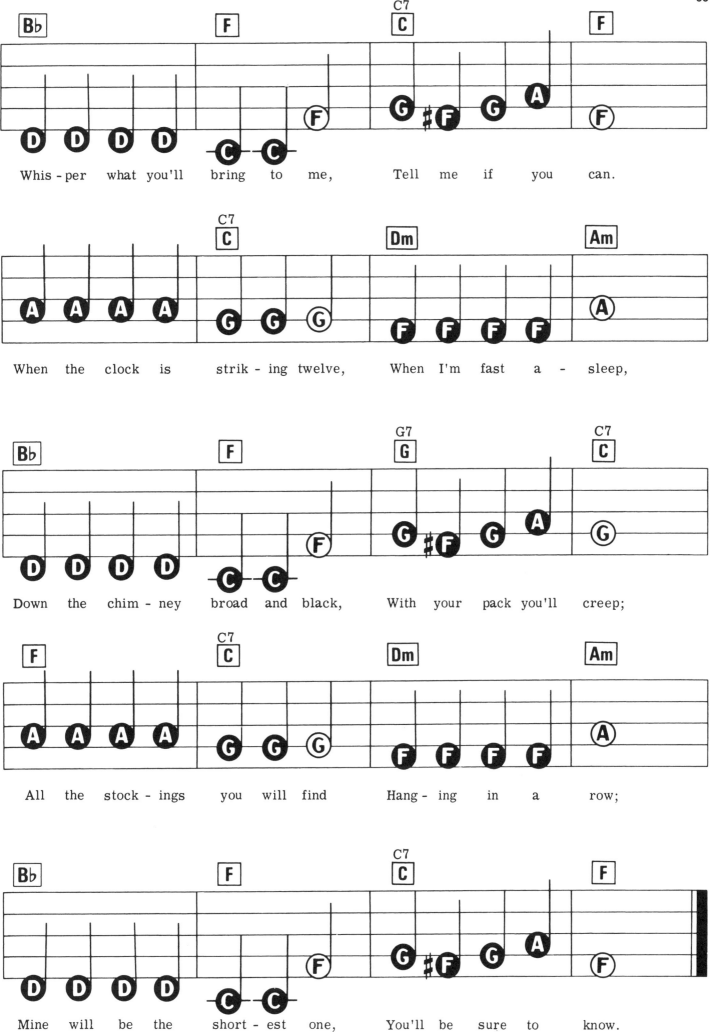

Joy to the World

Registration 6
Rhythm: March or None

Words by Isaac Watts
Music by George Frideric Handel
Adapted by Lowell Mason

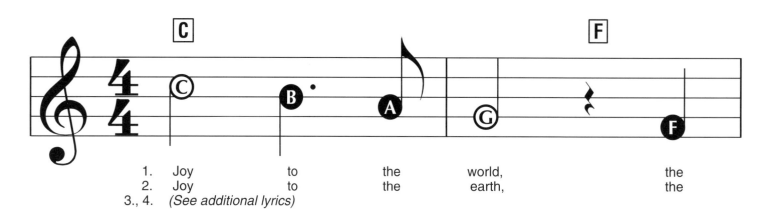

1. Joy   to   the   world,   the
2. Joy   to   the   earth,   the
3., 4. *(See additional lyrics)*

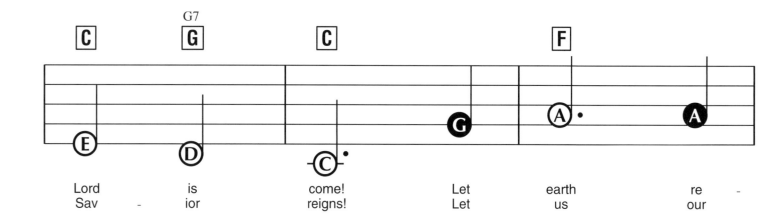

Lord   is   come!   Let   earth   re -
Sav - ior   reigns!   Let   us   our

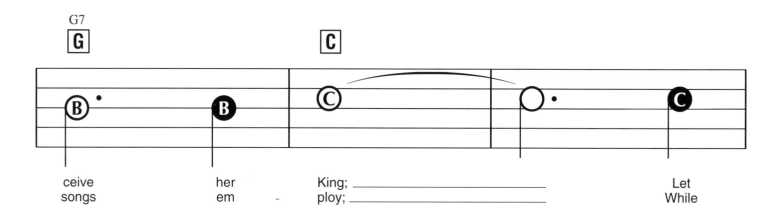

ceive   her   King; _____   Let
songs   em - ploy; _____   While

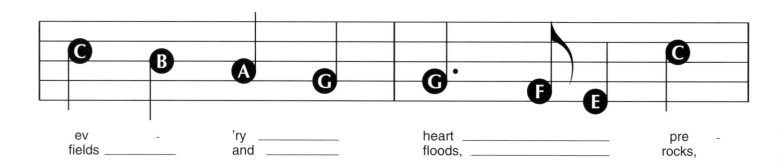

ev - 'ry _____   heart _____   pre -
fields _____   and _____   floods, _____   rocks,

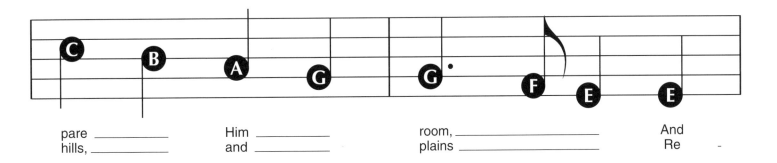

pare _____ Him _____ room, _____ And
hills, _____ and _____ plains _____ Re -

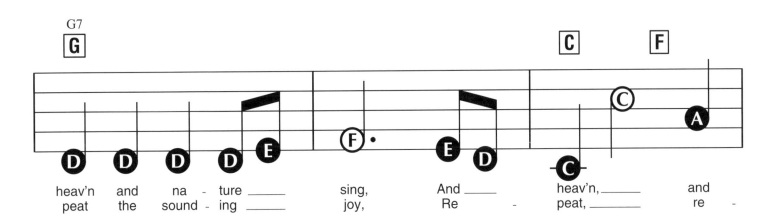

heav'n and na - ture _____ sing, And _____
peat and the sound - ing _____ joy, Re -

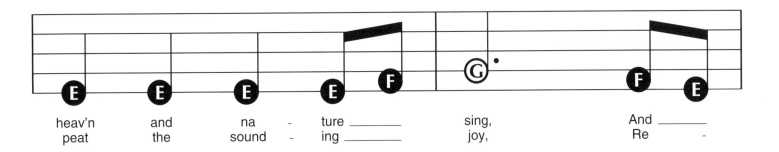

heav'n and na - ture _____ sing, And _____ heav'n, _____ and
peat and the sound - ing _____ joy, And Re - peat, _____ re -

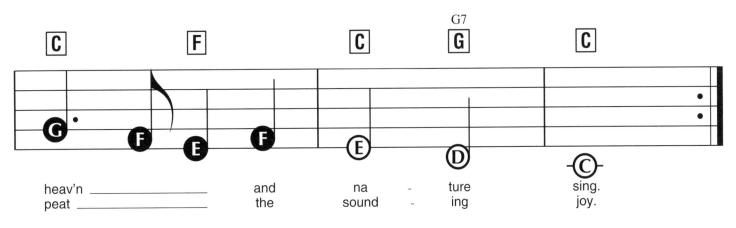

heav'n _____ and na - ture sing.
peat _____ the sound - ing joy.

Additional Lyrics

3. No more let sins and sorrows grow,
   Nor thorns infest the ground;
   He comes to make His blessings flow
   Far as the curse is found.

4. He rules the world with truth and grace,
   And makes the nations prove
   The glories of His righteousness
   And wonders of His love.

O Christmas Tree

Registration 3
Rhythm: None

Traditional German Carol

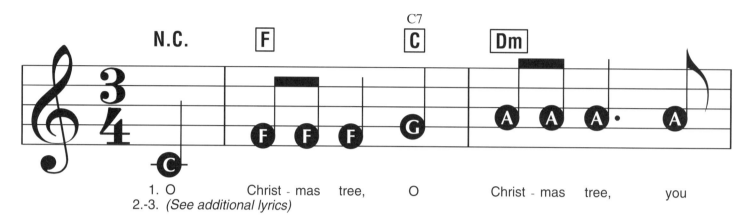

1. O Christ - mas tree, O Christ - mas tree, you
2.-3. *(See additional lyrics)*

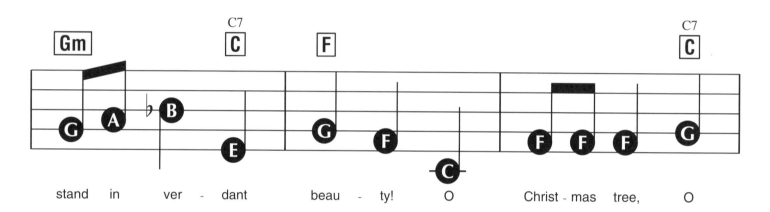

stand in ver - dant beau - ty! O Christ - mas tree, O

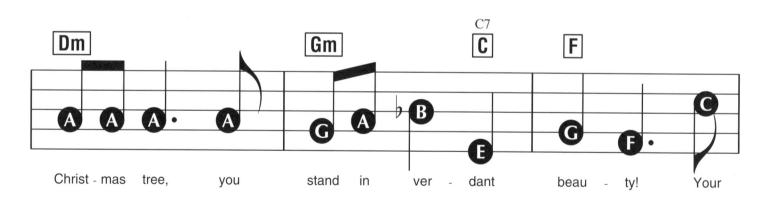

Christ - mas tree, you stand in ver - dant beau - ty! Your

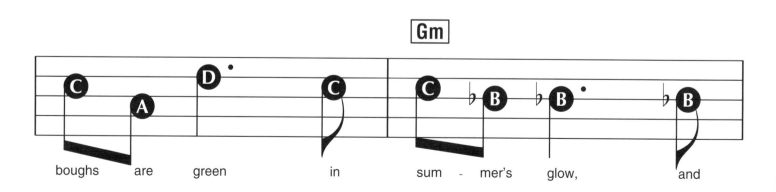

boughs are green in sum - mer's glow, and

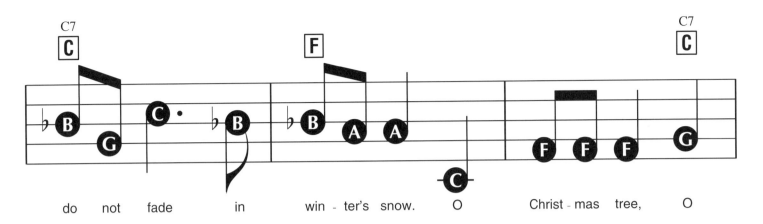

do not fade in win - ter's snow. O Christ - mas tree, O

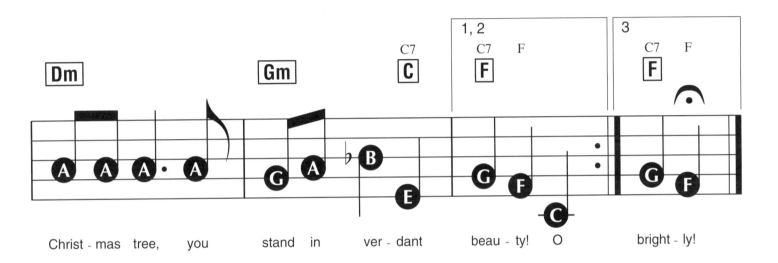

Christ - mas tree, you stand in ver - dant beau - ty! O bright - ly!

Additional Lyrics

2. O Christmas tree, O Christmas tree,
Much pleasure doth thou bring me!
O Christmas tree, O Christmas tree,
Much pleasure doth thou bring me!
For ev'ry year the Christmas tree
Brings to us all both joy and glee.
O Christmas tree, O Christmas tree,
Much pleasure doth thou bring me!

3. O Christmas tree, O Christmas tree,
Thy candles shine out brightly!
O Christmas tree, O Christmas tree,
Thy candles shine out brightly!
Each bough doth hold its tiny light
That makes each toy to sparkle bright.
O Christmas tree, O Christmas tree,
Thy candles shine out brightly!

O Come, All Ye Faithful

Registration 6
Rhythm: None

Words and Music by John Francis Wade
Latin Words translated by Frederick Oakeley

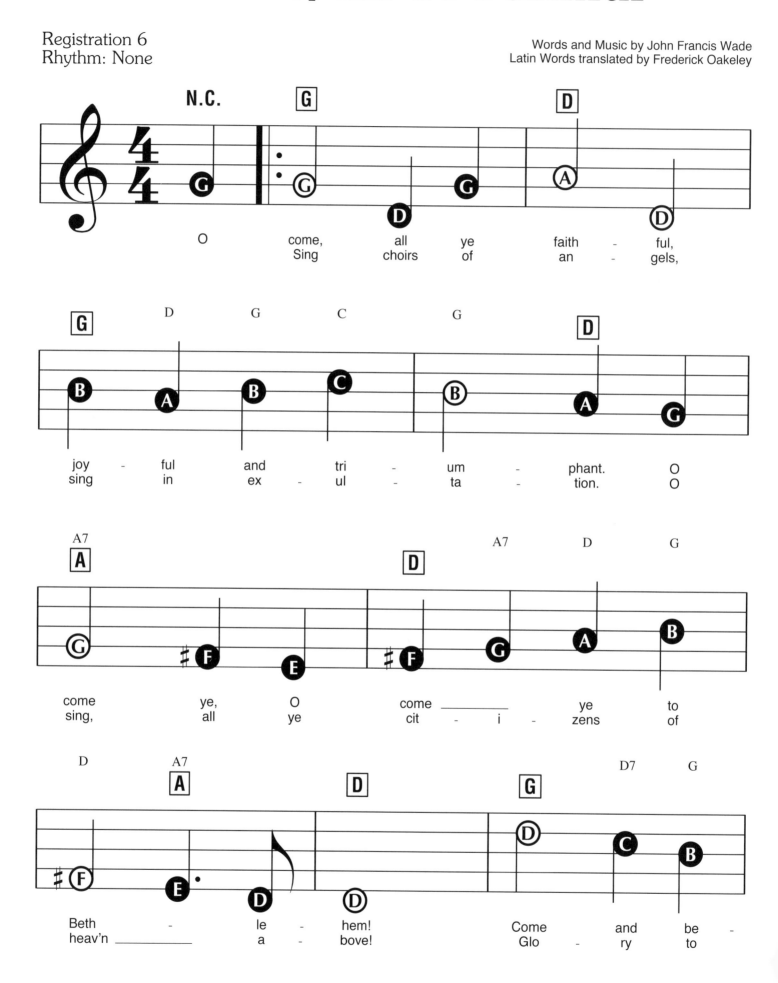

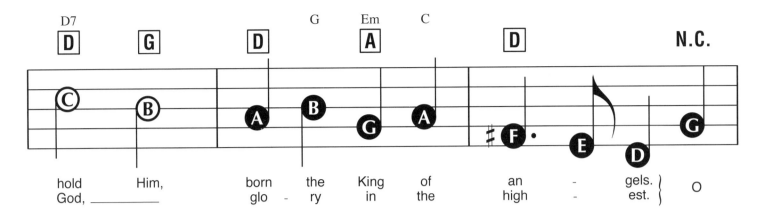

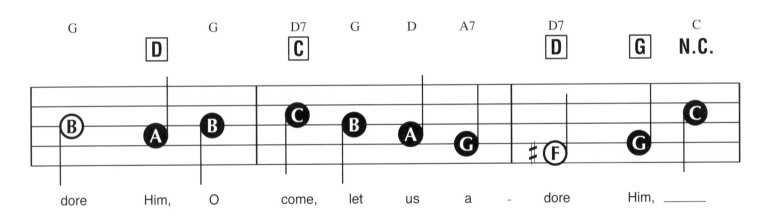

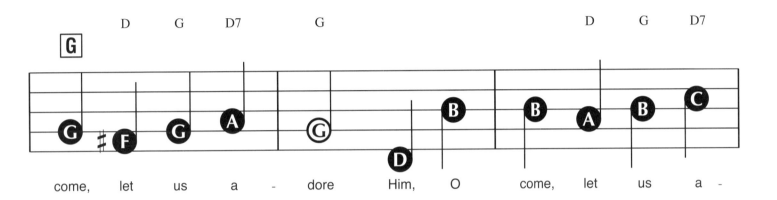

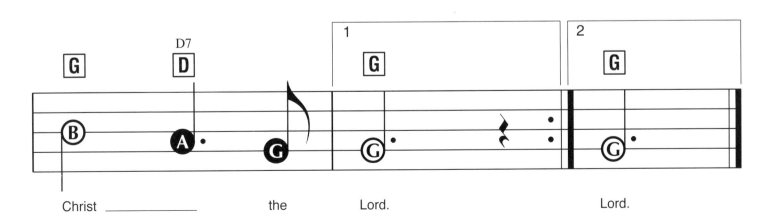

O Come, Little Children

Registration 1
Rhythm: 4/4 Ballad

Words by C. von Schmidt
Music by J.P.A. Schulz

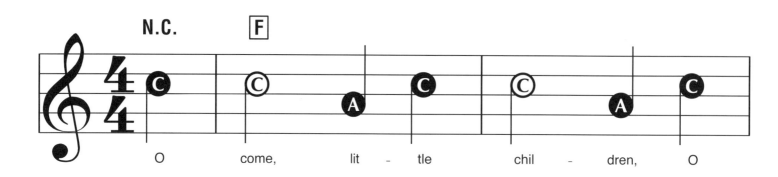

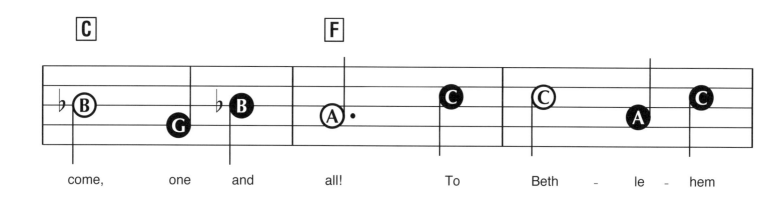

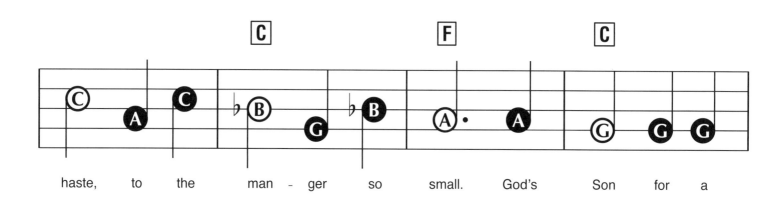

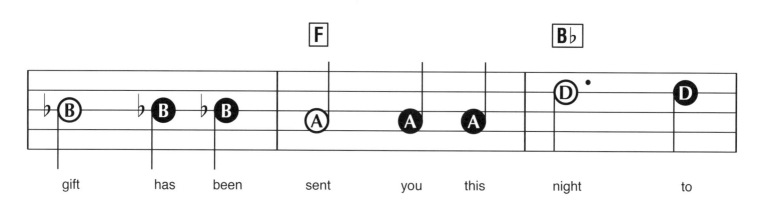

63

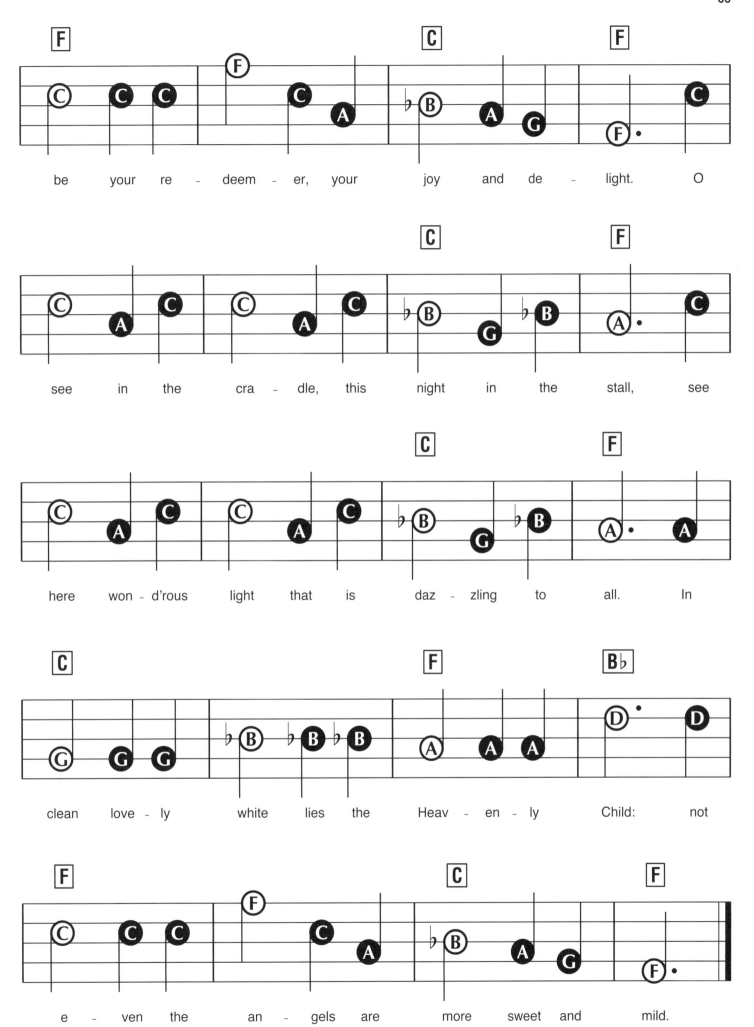

O Holy Night

Registration 6
Rhythm: None

French Words by Placide Cappeau
English Words by John S. Dwight
Music by Adolphe Adam

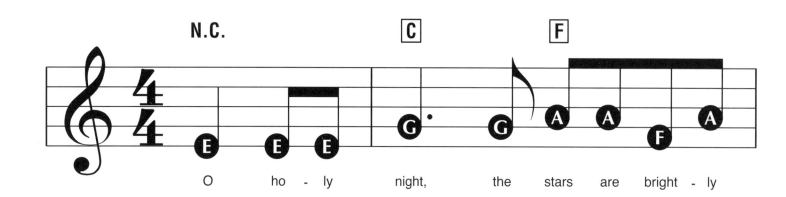

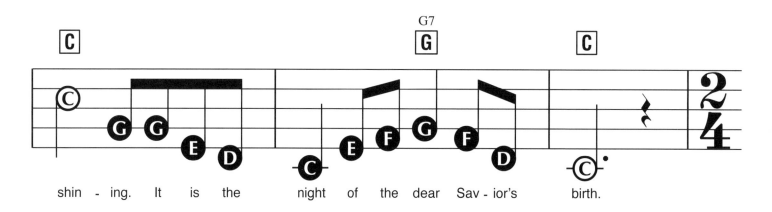

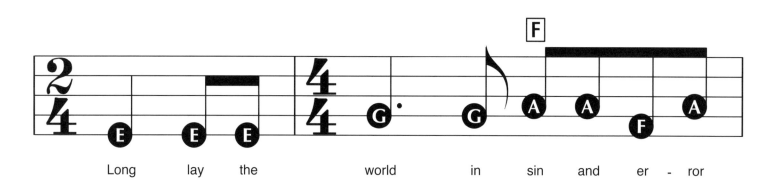

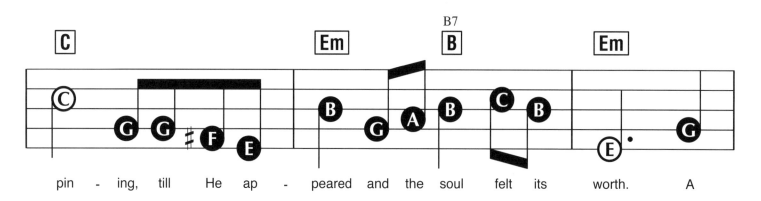

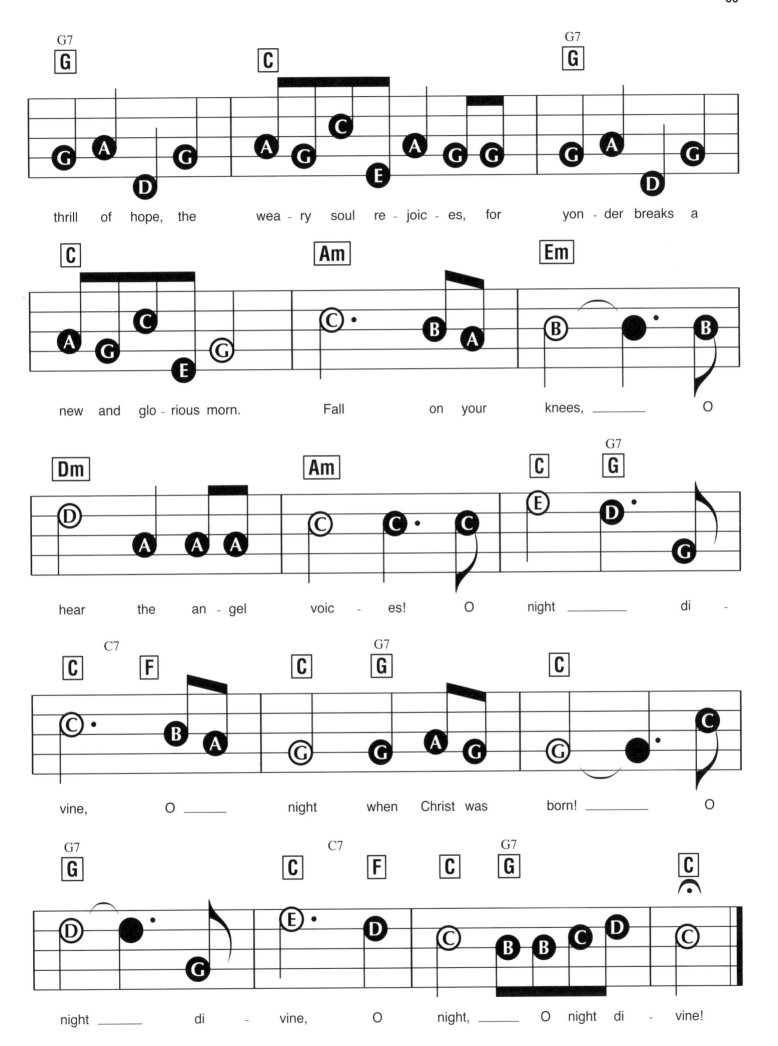

Silent Night

Registration 1
Rhythm: Waltz

Words by Joseph Mohr
Translated by John F. Young
Music by Franz X. Grüber

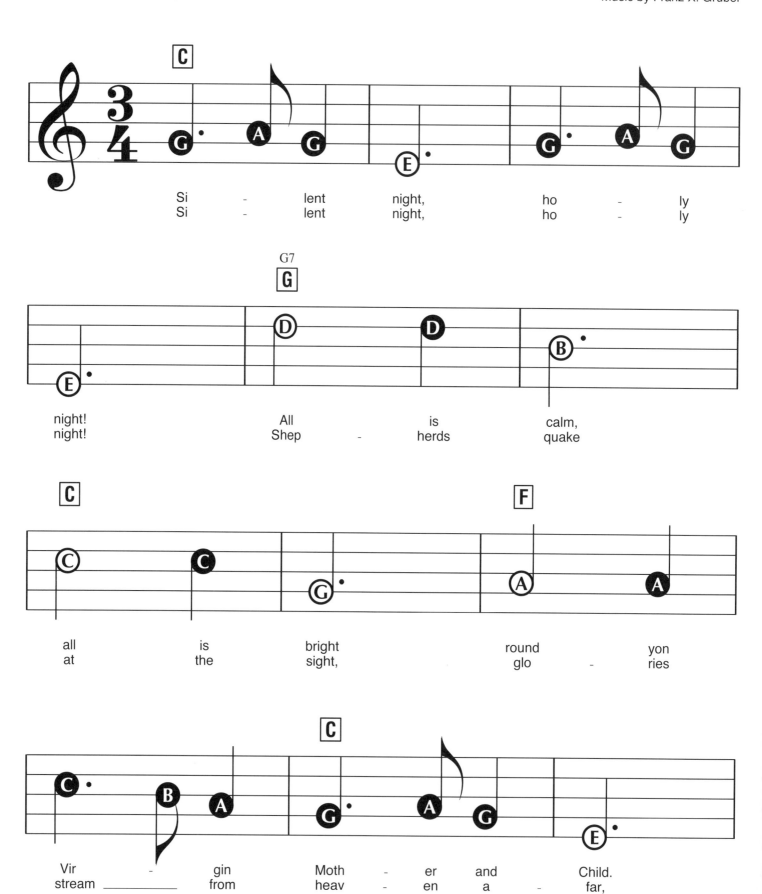

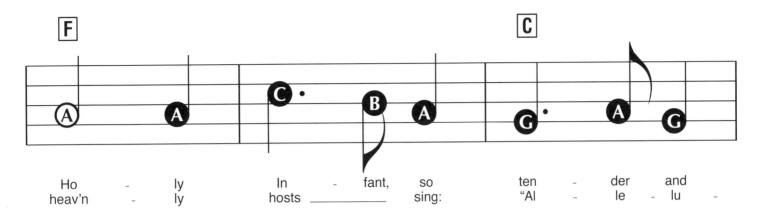

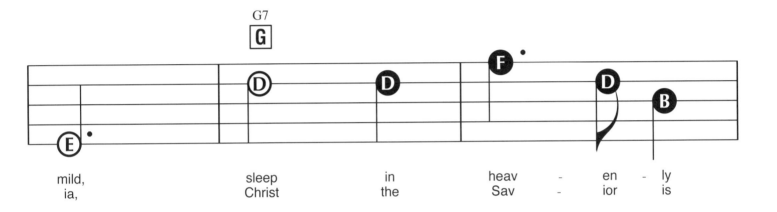

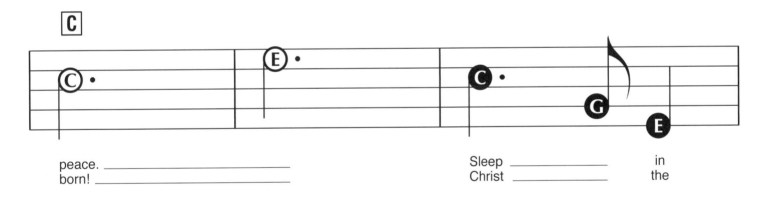

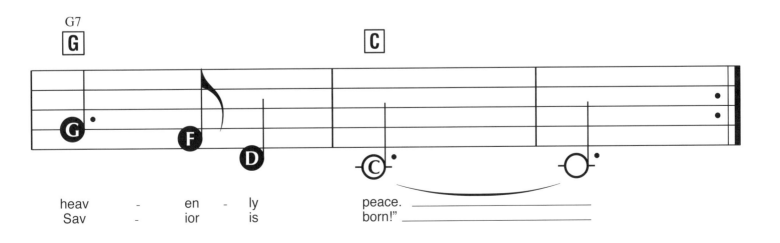

Toyland
from BABES IN TOYLAND

Registration 3
Rhythm: Waltz

Words by Glen MacDonough
Music by Victor Herbert

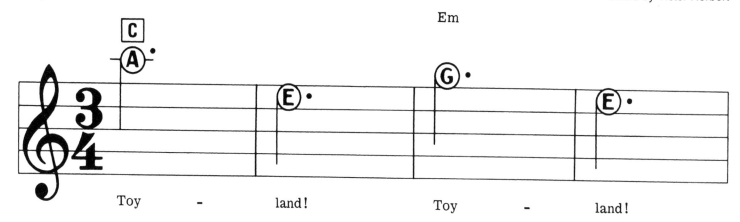

Toy - land! Toy - land!

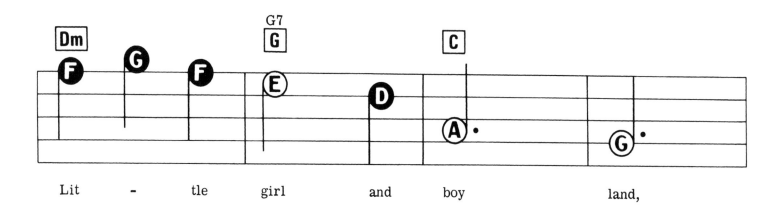

Lit - tle girl and boy land,

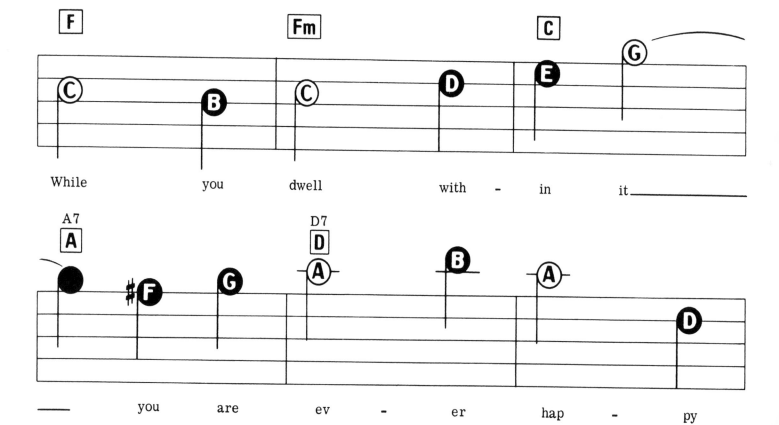

While you dwell with - in it_____

_____ you are ev - er hap - py

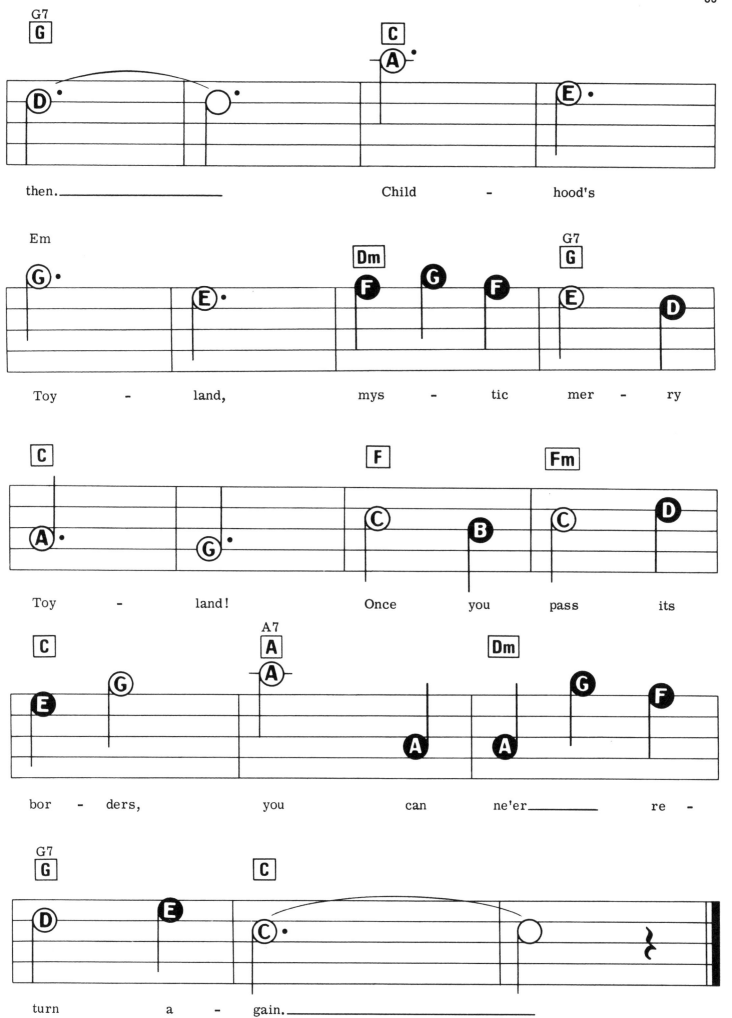

then._____ Child - hood's

Toy - land, mys - tic mer - ry

Toy - land! Once you pass its

bor - ders, you can ne'er_____ re -

turn a - gain._____

The Twelve Days of Christmas

Registration 5
Rhythm: None

Traditional English Carol

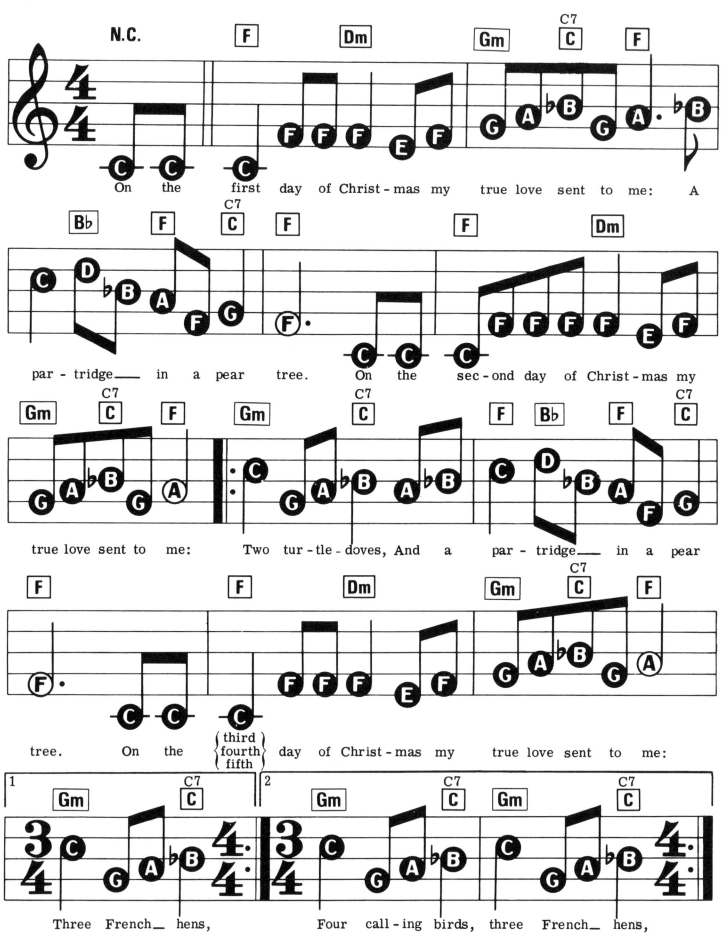

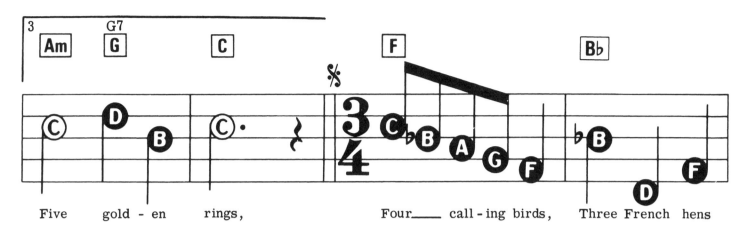

Five gold - en rings, Four__ call - ing birds, Three French hens

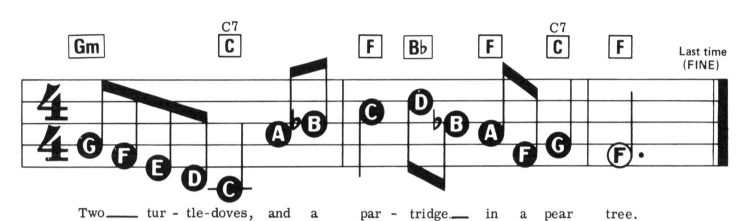

Two__ tur - tle-doves, and a par - tridge__ in a pear tree.

On the { sixth / seventh / eighth, etc. } day of Christ - mas my true love sent to me_____

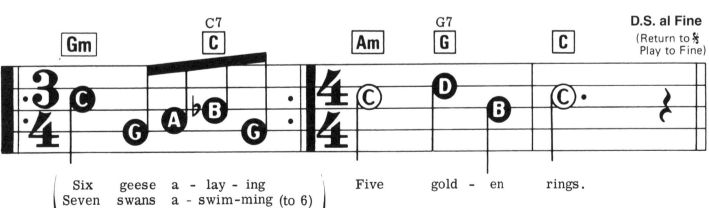

Six geese a - lay - ing
Seven swans a - swim-ming (to 6)
Eight maids a - milk - ing (to 7)
Nine la - dies danc - ing (to 8)
Ten lords a - leap-ing (to 9)
Eleven pi - pers pip-ing (to 10)
Twelve drum-mers drum-ming (to 11)

Five gold - en rings.

Up on the Housetop

Registration 2
Rhythm: Fox Trot

Words and Music by
B.R. Hanby

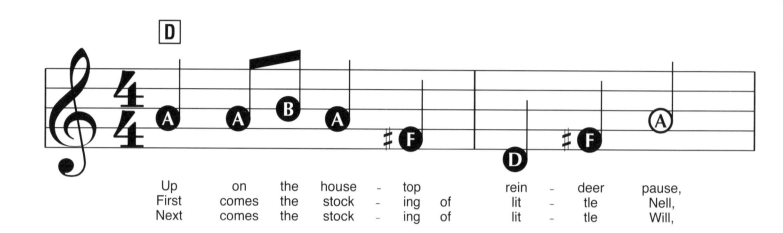

Up on the house - top rein - deer pause,
First comes the stock - ing of lit - tle Nell,
Next comes the stock - ing of lit - tle Will,

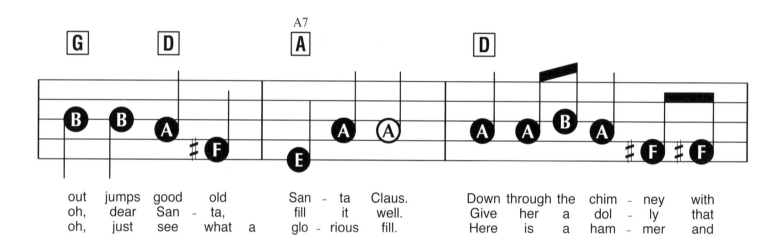

out jumps good old San - ta Claus. Down through the chim - ney with
oh, dear San - ta, fill it well. Give her a dol - ly with that
oh, just see what a glo - rious fill. Here is a ham - mer and

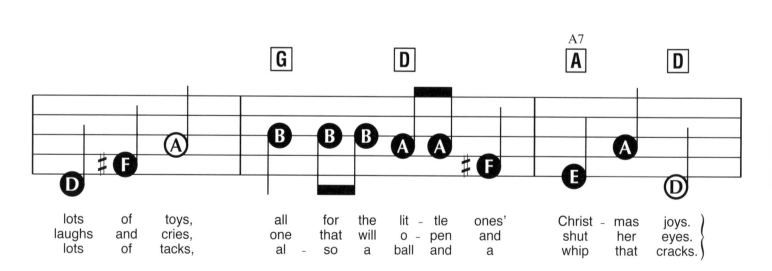

lots of toys, all for the lit - tle ones' Christ - mas joys.
laughs and cries, one that will o - pen and shut her eyes.
lots of tacks, al - so a ball and a whip that cracks.

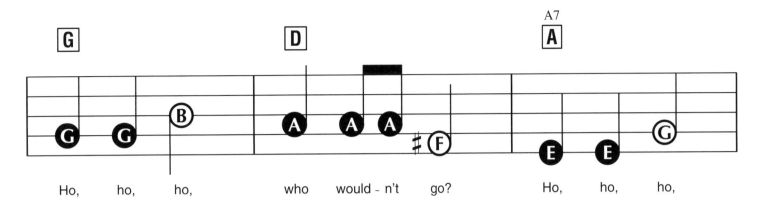

Ho,   ho,   ho,   who   would - n't   go?   Ho,   ho,   ho,

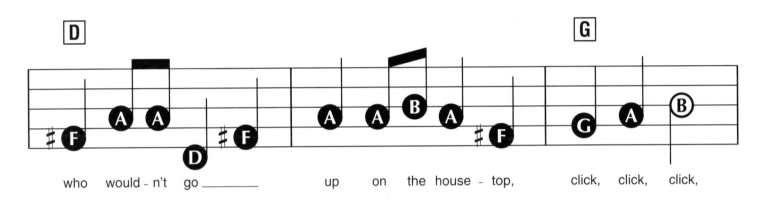

who   would - n't   go _____   up   on   the   house - top,   click,   click,   click,

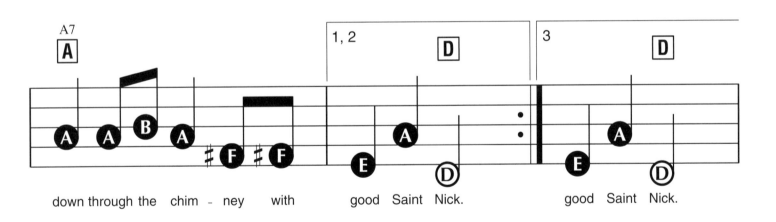

down through the   chim - ney   with   good   Saint   Nick.   good   Saint   Nick.

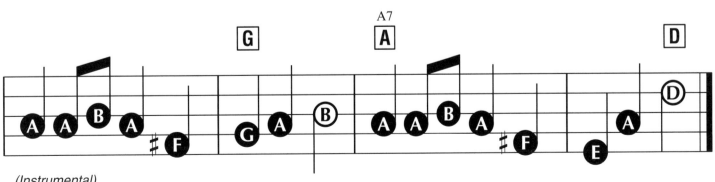

(Instrumental)

We Wish You a Merry Christmas

Registration 7
Rhythm: Waltz

Traditional English Folksong

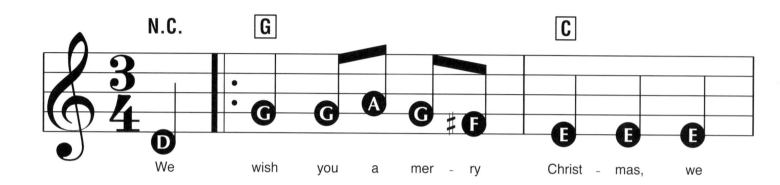

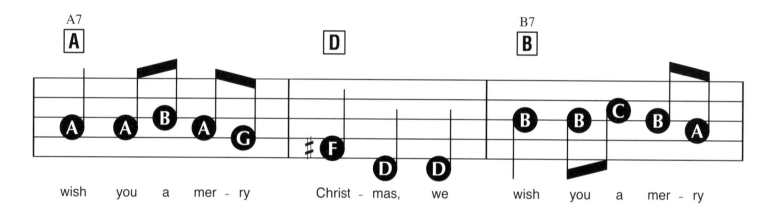

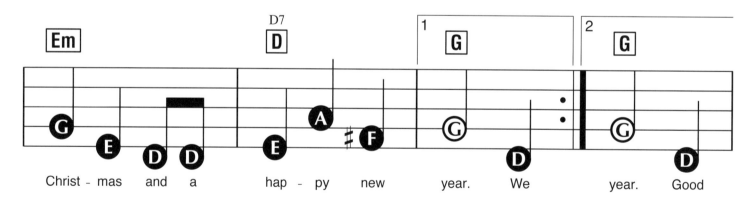

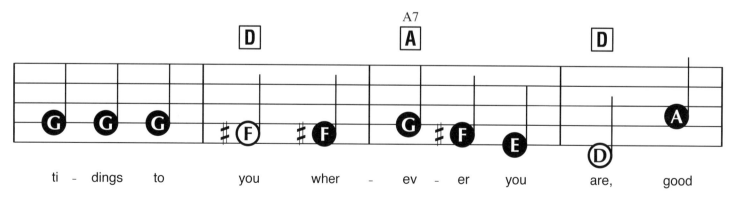

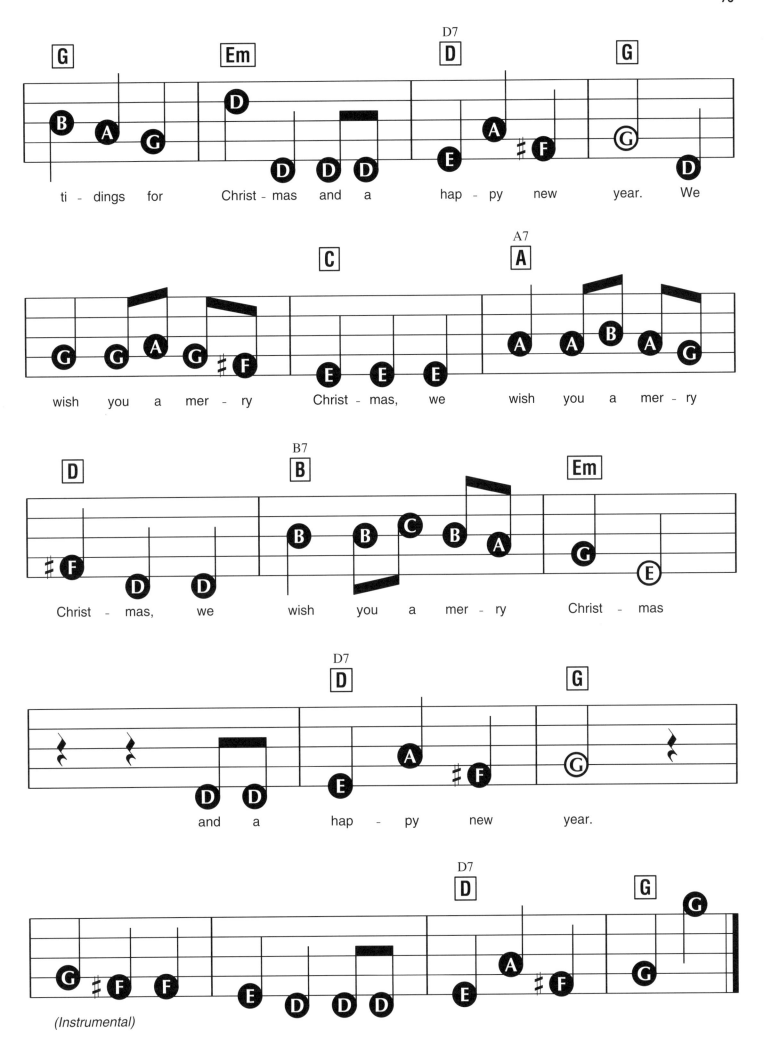

While Shepherds Watched Their Flocks

Registration 1
Rhythm: March or None

Words by Nahum Tate
Music by George Frideric Handel

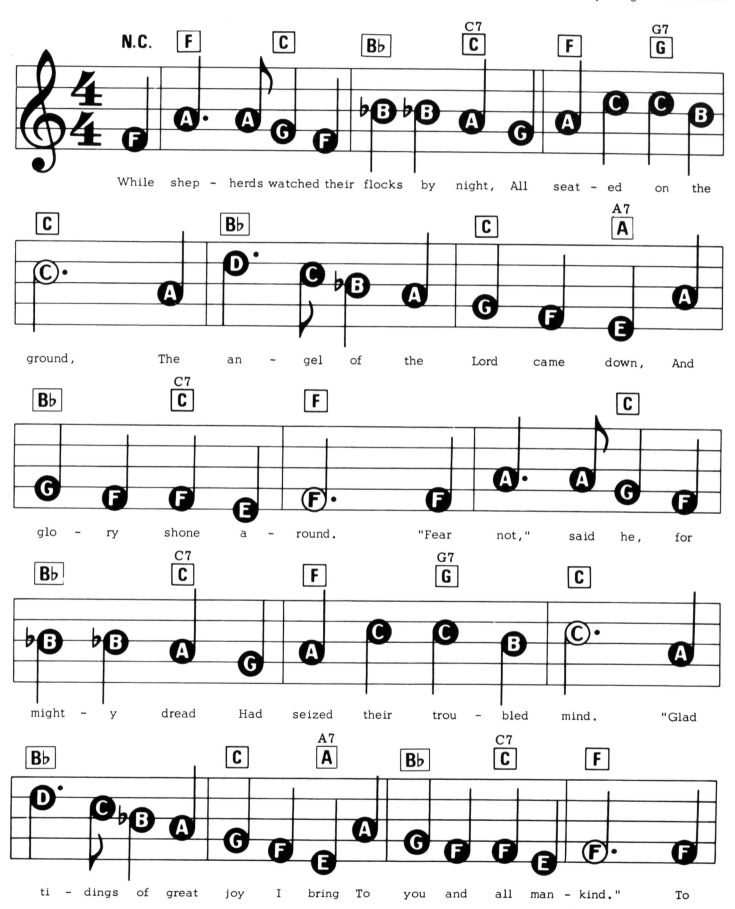

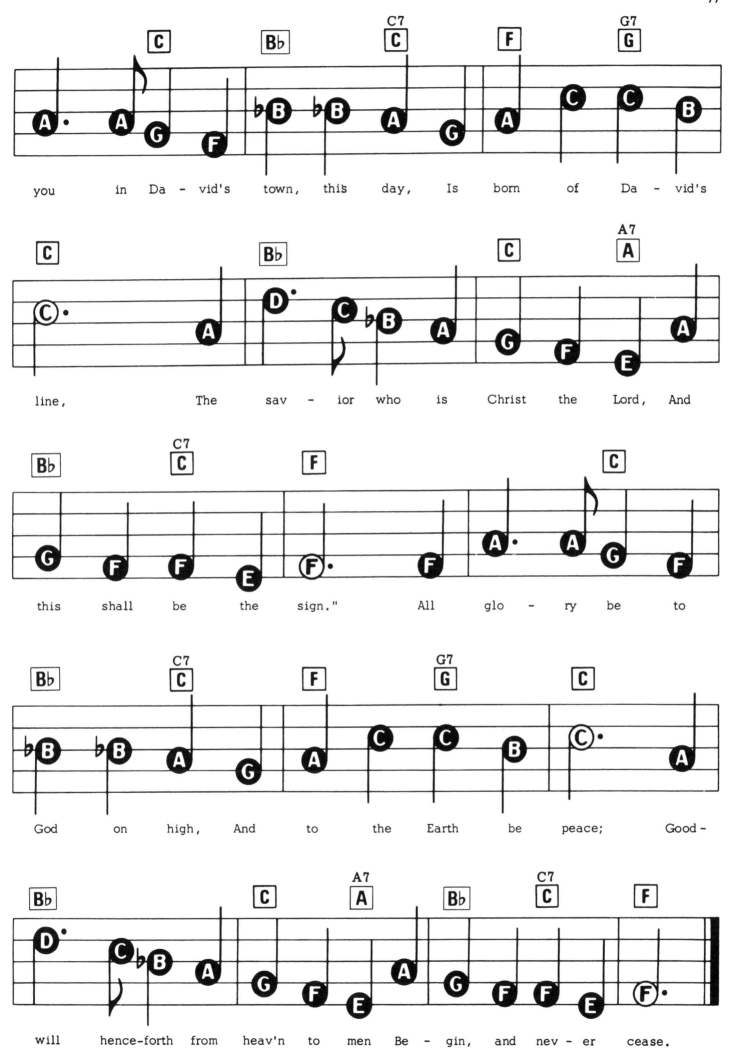

What Child Is This?

Registration 1
Rhythm: Waltz

Words by William C. Dix
16th Century English Melody

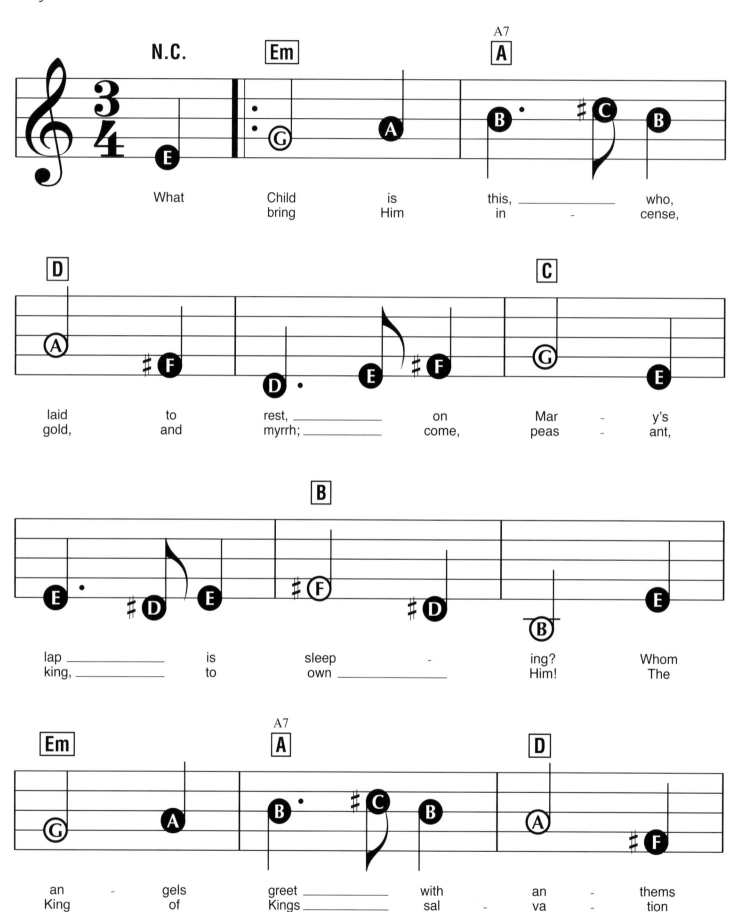

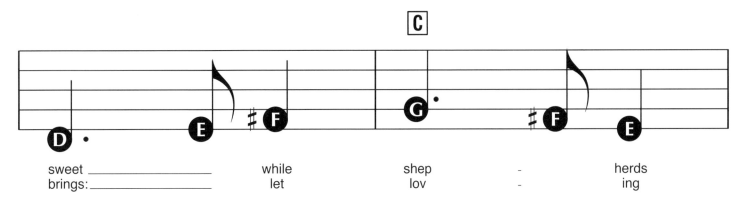

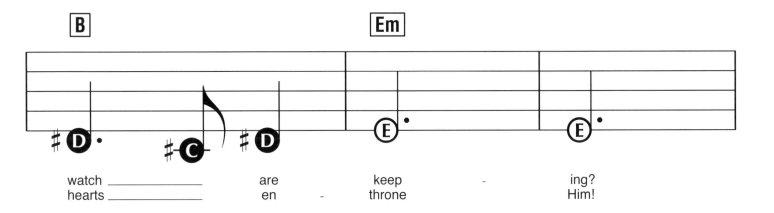

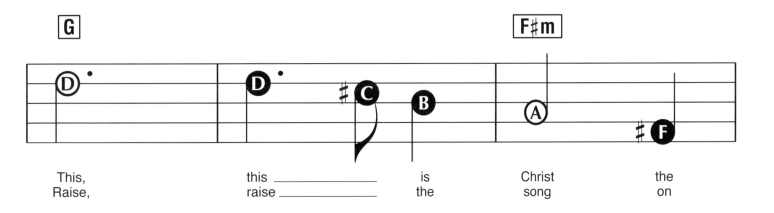

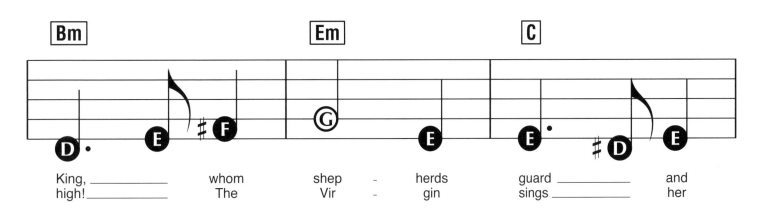

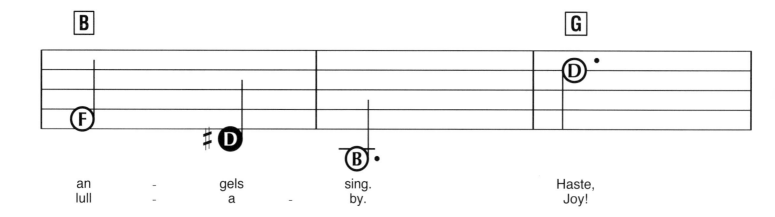

an - gels sing. Haste,
lull - a - by. Joy!

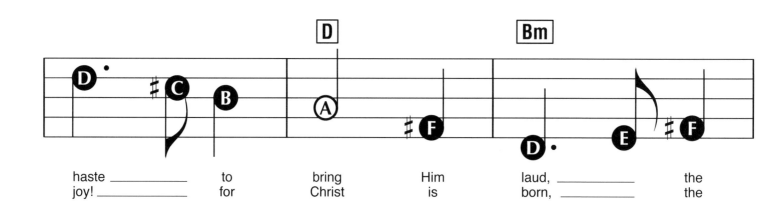

haste _____ to bring Him laud, _____ the
joy! _____ for Christ is born, _____ the

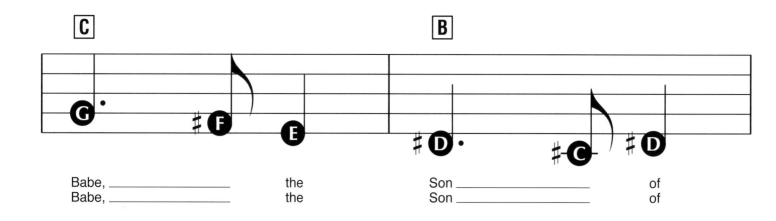

Babe, _____ the Son _____ of
Babe, _____ the Son _____ of

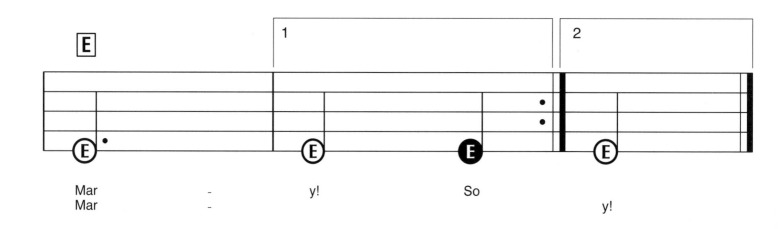

Mar - y! So
Mar - y!